COACHING SOCCER

THE OFFICIAL COACHING BOOK
OF THE DUTCH SOCCER ASSOCIATION

by
Bert van Lingen

Published by
REEDSWAIN INC

Library of Congress Cataloging - in - Publication Data

Van Lingen, Bert
   Coaching Soccer
      The Official Coaching Book of the Dutch Soccer Association

ISBN No. 1-890946-04-4
Copyright © 1997 Bert van Lingen
Library of Congress Catalog Card Number 97-075743

Reedswain books are available at special discounts for bulk purchase. For details contact the Special Sales Manager at REEDSWAIN 1-800-331-5191.

Printed in the United States of America.

IMPRINT

Author:	Bert van Lingen
Contributions by:	Vera Pauw en Rinus Israel
Author of goalkeeper coaching section:	Frans Hoek
Final Editing:	Vera Pauw
With thanks to:	Rinus Michels, KNVB technical advisor
With support of:	Henk van de Wetering (KNVB Academy),
	Ab van de Velde (KNVB-Drenthe),
	Joop Lensen (KNVB-Noord Holland),
	Albert Buisman (University of Utrecht)
Photographs by:	Jan de Koning / Ger Stolk
Translators:	ExperTeam Netherlands BV,
	Dave and Ilona Brandt
Editors:	Jerome and Miriam Hickey, Louisiana - U.S.A.
Art Direction/Layout :	Kimberly N. Bender

REEDSWAIN VIDEOS AND BOOKS, INC.
612 Pughtown Road • Spring City, Pennsylvania 19475
1-800-331-5191 • WWW.REEDSWAIN.COM

FOREWORD

Most top soccer players started playing the game when they were 6 or 7 years old. It speaks volumes for all the parents, volunteers, and club officials who have contributed to the development of budding stars - as well as lesser talents - as a result "tiny" Holland can regularly compete with the "giants" of the world's soccer nations.

One proof of soccer's popularity in the Netherlands is the active participation of so many people as players, managers, coaches, trainers, etc.

All those who are involved in the sport, and who may at some stage be privileged to play a part in the development of a future national player, will find this a stimulating and instructive book. Playing a role in the soccer development process of children is just as demanding and multifaceted as working with top players of the national teams.

We wish you every success in absorbing the knowledge contained in this book, and in translating it to your situation.

B. van Lingen

Table of Contents

INTRODUCTION

In 1985 the technical staff of the KNVB (the Dutch Soccer Association) in Zeist, under the leadership of Rinus Michels (its Technical Director at that time), decided to take a closer interest in the youth development policies of Dutch soccer clubs. It was found that the training tended to be focused on separate skills: individual technical skills (passing, dribbling, shooting, etc.), and on fitness training (running, jumping, etc). The technical staff of the KNVB analyzed all aspects of the soccer learning process. This resulted in, among other things, a renewed appreciation for street soccer. The most valuable elements of street soccer were molded into a training plan for youth soccer. The basic idea is that players learn by discovering the purpose, and aim of the game.

Games of 4 against 4, and variations of such games are used to achieve learning objectives. These games of 4 against 4 contain everything that made street soccer so attractive. Each participant sees a lot of the ball, and has to solve a lot of soccer problems, and there are plenty of goals and excitement. Such games incorporate all the key elements of soccer. A coach who accepts the philosophy that players should learn to play soccer by participating in real soccer situations must also accept that this has consequences for the manner in which his training sessions are organized. Objectives must be explained and players must be influenced while they play.

The coach can interrupt the game, give instructions, ask questions, encourage the players to make suggestions, give examples, get players to demonstrate what he wants to get across, or demonstrate it himself. The focus is on the qualities that players reveal during actual play.

Typical soccer activities are therefore central to each training session. This is the

Author Bert van Lingen

only way that players can become accustomed to solving a wide range of soccer problems and can learn to recognize these situations in a real match. The training activities are always geared to the age, skills and experience of the group. Each phase in the learning process of youngsters has its own coaching objectives (Chapter 4).

Players must be assessed during competitive play. How can a player make the greatest possible contribution while respecting the rules of the game? To answer this it is necessary to describe tasks and functions that have to be fulfilled during play. Such descriptions are naturally less detailed for younger players than for older ones (Chapter 11).

The sections dealing with this aspect are based on the so-called TIC analysis (Technical skills/Insight into the game/Communication with teammates and opponents) (Chapters 1, 4 and 5).

From the above it is clear that the results of tests (e.g. the Cooper test) are worthless as a basis for drawing conclusions about soccer ability. Such tests take no account of the competitive element. The main purpose of playing soccer is to win, not to demonstrate who can run furthest or fastest. Such considerations also throw a different light on fitness training for soccer players (Chapter 10).

The coaching of young soccer players advances from the simple to the complex. The coach proceeds gradually through a series of methodical steps that help players to improve their game. Organization and the introduction of structure into the learning process (during training sessions and matches) is very important if the complex whole is to remain comprehensible for young players. We refer to the rules which dictate the teaching/coaching process of children as the "didactics" of playing soccer (Annex).

The role of the goalkeeper is no longer treated separately. The goalkeeper is part of the team as a whole, and attention is focused on him in a number of forms. Frans Hoek, is a KNVB lecturer in goalkeeper training, and is also the goalkeeper coach of Ajax now at Barcelona Spain. He follows the same teaching principles as the technical staff of the KNVB.

To round everything off, a look is taken at the position of young soccer players within the soccer club (Chapter 11).

The ideas included in this book are aimed at the clubs. If the clubs are to profit from recent developments in (youth) soccer, it is essential that each club appoint a youth coordinator with a technical background, and allow him to sit in on board meetings. In this way the basic idea will be channeled into the (training of) coaches.

An important element of the implementation of the KNVB youth soccer policy in the Netherlands was the appointment of full-time district coaches. The KNVB has some 3000 associated clubs, distributed over 20 districts.

The KNVB coaches are responsible for developing a youth plan, scouting, selecting players, and promoting 4 against 4 (variations) in the clubs.

In addition the KNVB coaches support the training course policy at the clubs, and facilitate smooth communications between the KNVB and the clubs.

This book reflects the latest developments and the experience gained in recent years. Because it is intended as an accompaniment to a soccer coaching course, it takes the form of complete chapters, each of which can be treated separately without reference to the others. The fact that each chapter has to be able to stand alone means that some of the material is inevitably repeated.

We hope that this book will make a valuable contribution to your development as a youth soccer coach.

We wish you every success.

In 4 v 4, the situations are much clearer

CHAPTER 1
WHAT IS SOCCER?

Soccer is a game. One of the characteristics of a game is that the players can make choices, within the restrictions imposed by the rules. There is an element of freedom and, therefore, creativity. This is especially true of soccer. Soccer is a complex game. How could this be otherwise when so many players are involved - 11 against 11? In any given situation there are an infinite number of possibilities. All 22 players make their own choices, and the player with the ball also has to respond to these choices. Moreover, in contrast to sports such as basketball, in soccer the ball is "free". This means that the players of the team without the ball can try to take it off the player who is in possession. In days gone by the goalkeeper used to function as a "safe haven", but since the backpass rule was changed, playing the ball back to the goalkeeper has proved to be a dangerous maneuver, especially in the amateur game.

Because the ball is free, soccer is a game of constantly fluctuating situations, except when play is interrupted or the goalkeeper has the ball in his hands. These so-called "restart" situations provide the only moments in the game when play is static, and are therefore the only situations which can be rehearsed (free-kicks, corners, throw-ins, goal-kicks).

In a game such as basketball the player in possession is protected, and therefore every pass and movement can be rehearsed. Soccer players, in order to play effectively, must rely on their ability to recognize certain situations. These situations provide the only point of reference in the game. Players must know how to function in different positions when their team is in possession, when their opponents have the ball, and when a change of possession occurs. And all of this must be put into the context of the match, the competition, the pressure exerted by the opposing team, etc.

Soccer is all about winning. In order to win, one team has to score more goals than the other. A team can only score a goal if it is in possession, and it can only gain possession by taking the ball off its opponents. When a team gains possession it tries to build up an attack. If it loses the ball it tries to prevent the other team from scoring, by disrupting its buildup play and defending against an attack. These basic aspects are fundamental to any analysis of the structure of the game.

The elements on which the actual play is based, or rather the means by which the objective of the game, i.e. winning, can be achieved are summarized in the so-called **TIC** principle. **TIC** stands for:

Free-kicks can be rehearsed.

Technique:
This encompasses the basic skills necessary to play the game. No matter how small children are, or however elementary the standard of play, the players possess a certain degree of technical skill.

Insight:

Insight into the game is necessary in order to understand what actions are appropriate or inappropriate in a given situation. Insight is largely a question of experience and soccer intelligence.

Communication:

Communication in this context refers to the interaction between the players and all the elements involved in the game. This obviously covers communication with players of the same and the opposing team (verbal and non-verbal), but it also covers interaction with the ball (speed / weight / hard or soft, etc.), the field of play (flat / bumpy / wet / dry), the spectators (cheering / jeering), the officials, the coach, etc.

> **You have to have TIC to play soccer.**

TIC covers all the attributes needed to play and to influence the game.

An additional complicating and influencing factor is the continual flux of all these ingredients. Situations change continuously as the game progresses, and the players must repeatedly reorient themselves and make new decisions. The better a player's **TIC**, the greater his soccer proficiency. Aspiring soccer players must therefore aim to improve their technique, insight and communication.

In some games technique is all-important, and it can sometimes be an obstacle to the development of other attributes. For example, the technical skills required to be able to play field hockey are often a limiting factor which prevents youngsters from playing the game in a meaningful form. In other games, insight and communication may prove to be the limiting factors. The higher the standard of play, the greater the importance of insight and communication as factors in determining the game's outcome and how the team functions as a whole (team-building).

Many soccer players are simply looking for fun, amusement and relaxation. When soccer is played for enjoyment, there is no other objective than simply playing for its own sake. Soccer is fun, and that is justification enough. Each team may attempt to win, but the players are not interested in developing their skills; that is of secondary importance.

But soccer is also a sport, and sportsmen and women are usually driven by the ambition to improve their performance. Played as a sport, soccer has only one objective: winning. In order to win, obstacles must be overcome. All the attributes (TIC) which are necessary to play the game as well as possible must be improved. Soccer as a sport needs specialized training, aimed at improving performance systematically and methodically.

Furthermore, soccer is a competitive sport. Participants in competitive sports play against opponents, with the aim of defeating them and thus becoming a champion, or gaining promotion, or avoiding relegation. Competitive sport involves competition over a longer period of time.

The highest level of competitive sport is world-class sport. Qualification rounds and cup tournaments, such as the Soccer World Cup or European Soccer Championships, are part and parcel of the world-class game. However, it is not always clear where the line should be drawn between world-class sport and lesser forms.

Everyone experiences soccer in his or her own manner. For some, relaxation is the main aspect - sport for its own sake - while for others soccer is associated with an objective at a certain period of their lives. Some players even earn their living from the game.

What all soccer players have in common is that they play because they enjoy it. Whatever the case, soccer with its infinite possibilities is never likely to be boring.

CHAPTER 2
YOUTH SOCCER PLAYERS

Each and every one of us is different. This maxim applies in equal measure to adults, children and youth soccer players. Some people are reserved, others are outgoing. Some children are mistrustful whilst others are open and receptive to everything around them.

Getting along together is often a question of experience. There are no text books or manuals which give easy solutions on how to get on well with everyone, and that is just part of the problem facing a coach. Of course, this problem is not restricted to those who work with young people.

Anyone who is involved with children and young adults soon notices that certain behavior patterns are peculiar to certain age groups. However, this does not mean that all children in a given age group behave in the same way. Some children exhibit certain traits very strongly, others hardly at all. Behavioral characteristics surface at an earlier or later age in some children than in others.

The Dutch Soccer Association has divided youth soccer players into 6 different age categories: F, E and D beginners and C, B and A juniors.

The characteristics of a youth soccer player may be:

6 to 8 year olds: (F)

Easily distracted. Cannot concentrate for long periods. Too frolicsome to approach soccer as seriously as some parents might expect from them. Egocentric, no feeling for teamwork.

A typical feature of a game involving very young children is that they all want the ball, with the exception of the goalkeeper and one or two kids who have been repeatedly reminded to stay back in defense. It can hardly be called a proper

Even a teammate is an obstacle

game of soccer. The ball is rarely kicked cleanly, and it is chased around the pitch by a scurrying, flailing pack of enthusiastic youngsters.

When boys and girls have spent some time with a club the first signs of teamwork are noticeable. Although the ball may be kicked around more purposefully, the players abilities are largely limited to receiving passes, dribbling, kicking the ball forward, and shooting at goal.

8 to 10 year olds: (E)

Much more willing to participate in a team. Able to identify the difference between good, average and not so good players. Capable of practicing a specific drill for longer periods.

There is a noticeable improvement in ball control.

This is the ideal age for getting to grips with basic soccer skills. Skills are practiced with much more awareness and purpose than in the younger age groups. Teamwork takes the form of simple combinations. The concepts of marking and running into space are better understood.

10 to 12 year olds: (D)

Players of this age are more inclined to compare themselves with others. They are capable of pursuing objectives as part of a team. These youngsters have control of their own movements and work consciously at improving their game.

D beginners play in teams of 11. The basis for learning technical skills is already in place and the emphasis is now on developing insight into the game. In matches, players must accustom themselves to the size of the pitch, the rules of the game (e.g. off-side), playing to a specific system (e.g. 4-3-3) and, most of all, the principles of how to play when in possession and when the opposition has possession.

12 to 14 year olds: (C)

Increasing capacity to read the game. Development of individual opinions. Greater assertiveness. Increased tendency to compare own performance with that of others. Growth spurts can occur at this age, heralding the onset of puberty. Girls usually reach puberty before boys. In a relatively short space of time, girls may suddenly put on extra weight. Reasonable demands can be made on this age group with regard to the division of tasks within a team.

C players are primarily occupied with skills which began to develop in the previous age groups, i.e. running into space and marking. Heading duels are taken more seriously, with less of a tendency for the players to close their eyes when heading the ball. Improvements in defensive play are apparent. The number of instances when several defenders all try to deal with one opponent are less frequent. The responsibilities assigned to a particular position become clearer and are gradually absorbed.

	Objectives			Juniors		
	F	**E** **D**		**C**	**B**	**A**
	6　7　8	9　10　11　12		13　14	15　16	17　18
Age	Familiarity through play	Instruction by playing small sized games and basic games.		Instruction through use of all elements of a real match	Instruction by taking match performance as basis for coaching	Attaining optimal performance in training sessions and matches.
	Gaining control over the ball	Developing technical skills within the context of basic soccer games				
	The ball is the most important obstacle					
	Always in small sized games where each player gets as many ball contacts as possible	Always link technical skills to insight into the game and communication (TIC).				
		Accent: Technical development			Accent: Development and maturing of insight	

14 to 16 year olds: (B)

Boys become taller, which may result in a discernible decrease in their control of their limbs. In general girls have already reached full growth. Features of puberty such as apathy, stubbornness and moodiness are manifest in both boys and girls. Nevertheless, winning is more important than ever for boys. Girls seem more able to relativize the importance of winning. Some youngsters may take enthusiasm to extremes in their quest to discover how far they can push themselves.

B juniors are increasingly capable of playing genuine competitive soccer. Sometimes they try things which contribute little towards the team as a whole. Late sliding tackles, for example, or the way the ball is played with the outside of the foot, are signs that they are trying to prove themselves. The pace is faster and the marking is sharper. Players have to learn to cope under pressure, not always with success. Individual performances must contribute to the team's efforts as a whole, and this has to be learned.

16 to 18 year olds: (A)

More mentally and physically stable.

Players in this age group are characterized by a physical broadening of the frame and a more businesslike approach to what is happening around them. This is usually the age at which players decide whether to take up the game seriously or simply to continue playing it for fun.

The players are better able to deal with the problems encountered when playing in a limited amount of space. Although an A junior is not yet the complete soccer player, this is now simply a question of growing maturity. The restlessness which so typically characterizes B juniors is replaced by greater restraint. Players begin to pay attention to the way their team-mates play. A degree of self-discipline is acquired.

All this means that team managers and

The game looks the same.

coaches must be sufficiently aware of the idiosyncrasies of each age group. This will enable them to evaluate what can and what cannot be expected of their charges.

A game for girls too...

Up to the age of 12 the physical and mental development of girls and boys is roughly parallel.

Girls have the same attitudes to soccer as boys. Typical attributes associated with the F, E and D age groups apply as much to girls as to boys.

Girls' soccer is youth soccer.

For this reason girls are allowed to play alongside boys until the age of 14 and, subject to special permission, they may even play alongside or against boys up to the age of 16.

We speak of "mixed" soccer when all-girl teams or individual girls participate in a youth competition.

Experience has shown that mixed soccer has many advantages. The soccer development of girls who start to play soccer at the age of 6 is no different to that of boys.

As far as ball skills are concerned, children who take up a ball game like soccer at a later age are at a disadvantage in relation to more experienced players of the same age. Boys usually grow up playing with a ball, so many girls who join a soccer club at a later age are at a disadvantage in this respect.

This is the reason why ball control drills are preferred for girl beginners. Boys of the same age are generally more familiar with the ball, and as a consequence the girls tend to hold back more than the boys, who are inclined to show more initiative in their game. In Holland, one of the biggest problems facing girls' soccer (i.e. all-girl teams) is the fact that girls of 6 often have to play with or against girls of 15, because most clubs only have one girls' team. This means that the differences in levels of skill, ambition and appreciation of the game are too wide. In the younger age groups mixed soccer is becoming more common, so that begin-ners can play exclusively with and against players of the same age.

Puberty

From the age of 13 onwards, the differences become more evident. In general, girls reach the age of puberty sooner than boys. A girl will often adopt a nonchalant attitude as a form of protest against an adult who tells her what she can and cannot do. A girl knows best what she wants and what to do about it... or at least she thinks so.

Team managers at the club can turn this to their own advantage by involving girls in drawing up rules, organizing various activities, kit duty, etc.

Girls feel a need to justify their commitment to soccer. A surprising fact is that, in over-13 girls' teams, team-spirit is very evident and there is a will to succeed collectively.

These girls don't necessarily want to be the best. COLLECTIVE performances are felt to be more important than individual performances.

A talented girl playing in an all-girl team is not often keen on being singled out. This special attention may have the effect of lowering her performance, or she may even decide to change sports.

Only when a girl has acquired some maturity (17-18 years old) will she wish to view herself apart from the rest of the team and be able to accept being treated as a special case.

The difference with girls in mixed teams is striking. Girls in mixed teams don't differ widely from boys in their attitudes to the game. Chapter 12 goes into more detail on mixed soccer.

The team collectively achieved their goal.

CHAPTER 3

LEARNING HOW TO PLAY SOCCER

It is difficult to formulate a step-by-step approach to learning how to play soccer, because the learning process depends largely on practice. Soccer is learned by playing, and the time children spend playing the game is important for their soccer development.

Lack of time is probably enemy number one as far as learning to play soccer is concerned. Increased competition from other pastimes, e.g. other sports, computer games, television, etc., has had an adverse effect in this context.

Dennis Schup learned his tricks on the street.

In Holland, children used to spend endless hours playing soccer on the streets. They devised all sorts of soccer games, from scaled-down matches, to games which depended on the presence of walls, sidewalks and trees. This was how children mastered the skills of the game. The constantly changing circumstances stimulated their creativity: they had to adjust their play to the features in their immediate neighborhood, such as ditches, trees or the neighbor's yard (from which the ball might not always be returned). Progress went hand in hand with growing insight, sometimes referred to as "soccer intelligence".

Nowadays, however, soccer activities usually have to be squeezed into 1 or 2 hours of training each week at the local club, with games and drills which are devised, started and stopped by a coach.

Under the direction of Rinus Michels, the technical staff of the Dutch Soccer Association carried out a theoretical and practical study, on the basis of which they formulated recommendations on how children can best learn soccer in the few hours of practice time which are available each week.

If the time devoted to soccer were to be reduced still further the future of the game might be in doubt.

A positive approach is needed, and a range of high-quality soccer activities (training sessions and matches) must be provided. The lack of time devoted to learning to play soccer has to be compensated for by accelerated learning in a shorter period.

Conditions required for learning to play soccer

If this objective is to be realized, we need to know how children develop and what coaching targets can be set for the different age groups.

We must also analyze the game to discover how it can be simplified and made easier to learn.

In other words we should be asking ourselves: "What is soccer exactly?", "What sets it apart from other sports?", and "What ingredients can we identify?"

This analysis provides us with a basis for pinpointing the aspects which need to be emphasized at the different stages of a youngster's soccer "education".

At what age, and at what stage of the child's development, should the various aspects of the game be presented? What should take priority, and what are the phases of a child's soccer learning process?

In order to accelerate the learning process the 11 v 11 game needs to be simplified, but at the same time we need to retain as many typical features and characteristics of the game as possible:

Some players grasp it faster than others.

- Both teams can score
  ("What is the purpose of the game? What do we do when we have the ball, and what do we do when the other team has it?")

- Two teams play against each other from opposite ends of the pitch (i.e. the goals are located on the goal line and not just anywhere on the pitch).

- The pitch has fixed boundaries, so that the structure of the game is retained (direction of play; rules of the game).

These simplified basic games, sometimes referred to as small sided and competitive games, form the framework for the learning process and are extremely important in the education of young soccer players today.

However, given the minimal amount of time available for soccer practice, more is required. The quality of coaching in these basic games is a crucial factor in the education and development of players.

By making proper use of these simplified soccer games, a youth coach can accelerate the learning process of his young charges. A coach can help his player's development by passing on his expertise and skills.

The demands made on a coach:

A   The ability to "read" the soccer situation.

B   The ability to "manipulate" soccer obstacles (make them easier or more difficult, organize them in a methodical sequence).

C   The ability to explain clearly the problems involved.

D   The ability to provide the right example and to demonstrate it.

E   The ability to engender the right atmosphere for learning, and to stimulate a desire to do well.

The coach brings the simplified soccer situations (the basic games) to life, and uses the players' performances as a basis for coaching.

A few more points for consideration:

- Soccer clubs need a lot of people with soccer experience and insight. Lack of such a soccer background is a problem. Moreover, anyone who is involved in youth coaching should follow a specialized youth soccer coaching course.

- During training sessions with children, the coach should be able to empathize with the way the children experience these small sided and competitive games.

These simplified games reveal character, skills and shortcomings.

- Basic games are simplified soccer situations (small sided and competitive games) and they offer the best means of involving children in the game of soccer.

A youth coach must be able to manipulate obstacles flexibly (make them easier or more difficult) so that the children can progress methodically.

The most important objective in analyzing "learning to play soccer" is to accelerate the development of children's soccer potential by means of these simplified games and the associated coaching.

- Don't just duplicate the soccer games children used to play on the streets, but use well planned games derived from them, with as many soccer ingredients as possible, incorporating the useful elements of street soccer (similarities to "real" soccer, endless repetition, optimal enjoyment). On this basis, and taking account of their maturity and level of development (not to be confused with age!),
children should be allowed to play, and the coach should base his coaching on their performance.

Incidentally, this is the most difficult aspect of creating optimal learning situations.

- If the club is in a youth soccer league, the weekly match allows the children to demonstrate what they have learned. In this sense the match is a test. Of course the match is also an important means

"Talking it over..."

of promoting the children's soccer development.

Apart from the experience, the weekly match is an important moment in the learning process. Depending on the children's level of soccer development, a coach can emphasize particular aspects of the game.

The way in which the coach "uses" the match is important. At the very least the match should be geared to the children's ability to learn and understand (games of 4 against 4, 7 against 7).

. . . but the players have a role in thinking it through . . .

CHAPTER 4

COACHING YOUNG SOCCER PLAYERS

What is coaching?

Many people have struggled to answer this question. We shall keep the definition as short and simple as possible: Coaching is an activity aimed at influencing the way soccer is played and the people who play it.

Observe first and then act.

Observation

The basis of coaching is observation.

If a coach is to observe properly, he must not allow himself to be distracted by events around him which are not directly connected with the game. A coach should occupy his time by analyzing the causes and effects which determine the eventual outcome of the game. Shrewd observation and a good memory are fundamental to good coaching.

Coaching is usually a very personal matter. Forceful instructions are sometimes directed towards young players from the sideline. Jimmy is told to stay back, or Johnny to pass the ball quicker. It is questionable how much notice the youngsters take of all this, but it does represent an attempt at coaching. Of course, it might also be asked whether the result of the game would be any different if the instructor kept quiet.

Coaching the youngest age groups consists mainly of giving advice ("Throw the ball in from the behind your head, Tommy"). Coaching familiarizes boys and girls with how soccer is played.

"Tie your shoelaces properly, Billy, otherwise you'll trip up." There is a world of difference between this sort of advice and the first team coach's instructions to his striker to exploit an opposing defender's lack of pace. But whatever the age group, the coach must try to make a constructive contribution to his charges' development.

Should a coach be able to distance himself from the passions which arise during a game? The answer is yes, but this is easier said than done. A coach's view of a game must differ from that of a loyal supporter or even a neutral spectator.

A coach is not expected to experience a game in the same way as a dedicated fan. No one finds it strange if a fan becomes emotionally wound up, giving vent to whistles, whoops and yells of appreciation or disapproval. A coach, on the other hand, cannot afford such indulgences.

Does a coach have any emotions?

A coach has emotions like anyone else. However, youth soccer coaches have to take a long view. It is no coincidence that some clubs' first team squads include more products of their youth coaching schemes than others.

Two youth teams may be fairly even matched at a certain level of their development, but this is no guarantee that they will be equally successful in terms of the number of players who progress through to the first team. The work of the youth coach is often a crucial factor here.

The coach wants the players to pay attention.

Obviously a coach wants his team to win. Unlike parents and spectators, however, he regards winning as of secondary importance. His players' soccer development comes first.

A good coach sees a match in terms of clear objectives. Players are solely concerned with winning, but the coach regards competitive games as a means of promoting the development of his players. He therefore has other, less immediate, objectives.

During a match a coach will take the necessary measures to achieve a good result. Sometimes his aim will be to achieve a victory for his team, and sometimes it will be to promote an individual's development as a player.

A coach must not allow his enthusiasm to run away with him, and impair his ability to observe and assess. The coach therefore has a different role to that of the supporter, the referee or the club president.

Spectators are passive observers who express their approval or disapproval as the game progresses. The coach, however, is an active observer. He sees details that escape the ordinary spectator. There is a difference of emphasis on the importance of cause and effect. Most spectators make judgements based on effects (the end result), but coaches focus primarily on causes. For example, an outside right may beat his man and get to the goal line before cutting the ball back to the incoming center forward. The crowd is only interested in the result of the move, and responds with mixed feelings when the ball goes behind the intended recipient. Both coaches, however, are more concerned with analyzing the whys and wherefores of the situation.

The coach of the team which almost conceded a goal asks himself why his left back was beaten so easily. Did he allow the outside right to get too close? Was he properly balanced so that he could react alertly and try to win the ball? Was he too easily deceived by his opponent's body swerve? Where was the sweeper? Why was there no cover at the back, and how could the center forward turn up unmarked in front of goal?

The coach of the team which almost scored wonders whether his outside right needed to go through to the goal line. Perhaps he should have played the ball square a little earlier. Having reached the goal line, where he was under no pressure, maybe he should have waited a little longer before crossing. Perhaps the center forward came in too fast, causing him to overrun the pass. Or a defender may have given the center forward a push at the crucial moment.

These are the thoughts which run through a coach's head in the first few seconds. Obviously a game of soccer is full of such incidents. These incidents give a coach ample opportunity to observe and assess the performance of individuals and the team, and try to effect improvements.

First of all explain the broad outlines.

Similar situations can often be reconstructed in training sessions. Sometimes a single remark might be sufficient to ensure a different outcome in a subsequent match.

Sometimes the coach is the only person in the group who needs to take the long view. He must look beyond today's game, whether lost or won, to the next training session or match. What went wrong today must go right tomorrow. And - just as importantly - what went right today must be emphasized and reinforced.

It does happen - all too frequently - that a youth coach sacrifices the development of a particular player for the sake of the team as a whole. One instance of this is when, for example, the team's best player is told to play as sweeper in order to strengthen the defense. Or sometimes a player might be given strict instructions not to go forward, even though that is his natural inclination. It is obvious that such a player will lose his enthusiasm and that his development will stagnate if his natural instincts are always suppressed and he is only allowed to participate when the opposing team is in possession. Many talented youngsters have thrown in the towel because they were forced to play as their coach dictated.

On the other hand it is clear that youth soccer is particularly suitable for allowing, for example, a striker to gain experience as a defender. The purpose of this is not to turn him into a defender but to make him more complete, as both a soccer player and a striker. Since the outcome of a game is, relatively speaking, less significant in the younger age groups, it is the job of the youth coach to take the first steps in this direction.

The coach will find that his efforts in this area will be appreciated. Giving a youngster the chance to play in another position often has a positive effect.

This can also cause a few surprises. Frank de Boer of Ajax Amsterdam started his career as a striker but is now a Dutch international defender.

None of the above is meant to imply that a coach should give the impression that winning and losing are irrelevant. A coach who relativizes the importance of winning, and finds that this brings him into conflict situations, must be able to appreciate that this is part and parcel of the players' development process. Most young players do feel that winning is very important, and are best served by an inspirational coach who remains enthusiastic and optimistic.

Learning to coach

There's nothing more practical than good theory.

It must be assumed that coaches are well intentioned. Sometimes, however, a coach is not fully prepared for the job. Maybe he has been talked into it, or regards himself simply as a stopgap. Or he may be a famous former player who feels that coaching youngsters and accompanying them during their matches is a piece of cake. Such coaches are sometimes successful, but more often than not the former player ends up being quoted in the press as saying that today's youth has the wrong attitude or has no backbone.

As if nothing had changed since the famous soccer player was young, and today's youngsters were faced with the same educational and other demands as he was!

Coaching has to do with the experience gained in all sorts of situations. You can only learn through experience. Sometimes a coach will suddenly realize that he judged a situation wrongly a number of years ago. As a result of his subsequent experience he is now able to appreciate this.

A coach must remain self-critical. He must be able to judge himself just as critically as he judges others. Did he do his job well? How did his players respond? Did he get the response he expected when he made his comments? If not, what should he have said?

The development of a coach can be equated with that of a player.

Is the problem recognized as such?

A lot of it has to do with the enjoyment he experiences. And obviously the better a player's success, the greater the coach's satisfaction.

Learning to coach can be divided into 5 different phases:

1. Knowledge and understanding of the game.

First and foremost the coach must be familiar with the ins and outs of the game: What do we do when we are in possession? What do we do when the opposition has possession? What demands are made on the players in their different positions?

2. Reading the game

This means: seeing what happens and listening to what is shouted and said. The ability to look and listen, i.e. observe, is a fundamental requirement for every youth coach. A coach who can detach himself and concentrate on what he sees and hears will be able to perceive more than others. This demands effort. After all, a coach has to divide his attention to events before, during and after a training session or match. Here are just a few examples of what might go through a coach's mind:

"....So, the tea has been organized for half-time....Is Steven warming up with the others?....Carlos has a good left foot, he'll be a pleasure to watch....Pete is pushing up well as last man. That wasn't what we agreed but it's working out well....Simon's daydreaming again; late to bed I suppose....Pedro's going into those heading duels with his eyes closed....Jack should tie his shoelaces better....Watch out! The water bag's falling over....Ted's not enjoying being the linesman....At long last, Frank I is finally learning to beat his man....Frank II still hasn't grasped when to come out....Clint's corners; remember that someone must stand at the near post....Leon's long passes could be more

accurate....Heck, the marking at the back is slack....Why aren't the midfielders helping out in defense....The strikers are standing around like statues today...."

And so it might go on. It is a good idea for a coach to draw up his own list. This is a good exercise. He might then realize that there are more soccer problems to solve than he had imagined. When a coach realizes this, he will immediately recognize that he has been neglecting a number of essential points, and that there has been no consistent line or structure to his coaching.

3. Objectives

A number of items he jots down will no longer be important once the training session or match has finished. Some others will be worthy of more detailed consideration and an attempt should be made to turn them to advantage. The coach should ask himself how he can contribute to solving soccer problems.

We refer to the coach's answers to these questions as his objectives, irrespective of whether they are concerned with eliminating specific deficiencies of the team and individual players or with exploiting specific skills more efficiently.

Knowing what's going to happen.

4. Setting priorities

The more experience a coach gains, the more soccer problems he will encounter. The wider his experience, the better he will be able to set priorities.

Training sessions are usually restricted in length. This means that a coach cannot work on all his objectives at once. Sometimes a minor problem may need to be solved before a major one can be.

For instance, the coach of a team of 10 to 12-year-olds will need to jot down a number of points for his own reference. Before he discusses aspects such as defensive covering, switching positions or the positional play of the midfielders, he will first have to make sure that his players all know where they have to play, in for example, a 4-3-3 formation. Solving one problem in soccer inevitably raises the next. This is a sign that the team is progressing.

The youth coach must know which of his objectives takes priority. This applies in respect to individuals, groups of players and the whole team. The coach decides which problem should be tackled first and which ones can wait.

If a coach fails to set priorities and attempts to cover everything at once, this is a sign that he is unable to understand how youngsters experience the game of soccer. In practice such a coach will be less successful than his colleagues who do set priorities.

Of course each age group requires its own objectives. Certain aspects of the game need to be emphasized in a certain way at a certain age. There is therefore no need for the coach to reinvent the wheel.

5. Planning

From the above it is clear that a coach must work methodically. A wise coach will make a plan of action for the whole year at the beginning of each season. Such a plan must outline what the coach expects to achieve by the end of the year and how he intends to do this.

The coach must be aware of his players' current level of soccer skills. He must also define the level that he expects the team to have reached at the end of the season. This will be reflected in his planning, which will also incorporate his priorities.

Depending on the coach's personal preferences, short-term plans can also be drawn up, for three months or even one month for instance. We have summarized the different aspects of coaching in a model which we refer to as a phase plan. Reality, even that of a soccer player, is usually extremely complex and impossible to describe completely. If we wish to exert an influence we will inevitably have to accept some level of simplification. A model is therefore used to facilitate an understanding of all the aspects involved.

A coaching model

It should be evident by now that the coaching of young soccer players is not something which can be taken lightly. The coach must decide beforehand what he wants to get over to his pupils in the next training session.

Planning and preparation are essential to coaching. Once a session is over, a coach needs to assess how it went and what results were achieved. We refer to this as evaluation. The following so-called "Van Gelder" model provides the soccer coach with a number of options which he can adapt for use in the context of his own activities.

The Van Gelder model is based on the following key questions:

1. Where should I begin?
   (starting point)
2. What do I want to achieve?
   (objectives)
3. How can I coach?
   (how and what/resources)
4. What results have I achieved during the training session?

Coaching before and after the game.

The content of the coaching can be based on different concepts of how to deal with youngsters. In the concept of the Dutch Soccer Association the child occupies center stage. In other words, we create conditions in which children can begin to act independently. As far as coaching before and after the match is concerned this means:

Before the game:

Youngest players

- Let them blow off steam by allowing and encouraging them to play with the ball (e.g. a sort of preliminary warming up, which can be developed further at a later age).

- Encourage the children to change into and out of their kit in the changing rooms and to try to be independent (allow parents to help in the changing

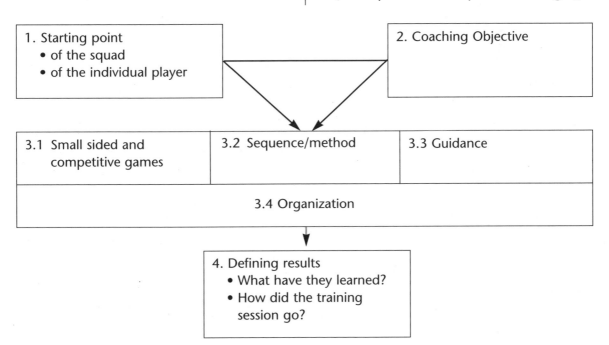

This model is described in detail in the Annex (instructions and method).

room as long as the children need them).

- Comments on the game should be formulated simply, for example: "As soon as the other side has the ball, try to win it back again. And remember all of you, no waiting for the ball to come to you, and no hanging back."

If children can hardly tie their own shoelaces, they can't be expected to replace a broken lace.

Older players (e.g. 14 to 16 year olds)

- Use the previous game as a basis: "I want more teamwork this time. You're losing the ball too often because individuals are trying to do too much on their own when there are too many opponents around them or there's not enough space.

- Talk to each other about the tasks which have to be carried out during the game.

- Monitor the warming-up routines which the players have been taught to carry out without supervision (if necessary take corrective action or emphasize certain aspects).

During the game

Youngest players

- General instructions which are related to previous situations (training sessions/matches/discussions)

  For example: "Take the ball towards the goal", or "Go and win the ball".

Older players

- Remarks in relation to match performance, aimed at influencing individuals and the team in order to achieve a given result.

- For example: "Don't go into situations on your own when no-one is helping out. Ensure that your opponent remains boxed in. Win the ball back". Or: "You can't play at such a high tempo all the time; that's why you keep losing the ball. Try to retain possession and build up your moves more calmly."

  N.B.: Before giving instructions, encourage the players to analyze problems themselves and come up with their own solutions.

After the game
Youngest players

- Begin by summarizing your impressions of the game: "You did well today. We had a lot of possession, but next week we'll have to try scoring more than just the one goal we got today. We'll work on that during the next training session."

- "Go and have a good shower. And knock the mud off your boots before you go into the changing room"

"Good tackle" - a constructive remark by the coach.

Older players

Comments on the positive and negative aspects of the game must be made clearly so that everyone understands them. Don't be afraid to name names. Let the players talk about their own or their colleagues' performances first.

- Try to link up with the aspects which were discussed during or after training sessions.

- Work on individual aspects of the game, e.g. passing the ball repeatedly to the wrong flank, mistimed heading duels, lack of communication on the field, etc. Emphasize the good points as well, e.g. a good cross, a well-taken short corner, a clever free kick, a good way of approaching the referee, etc.

Substitution

- Try to avoid leaving players on the side-line in the youngest age groups.

Talk with the opposition coach and try and give everyone a game (e.g. 9 v 9).

- Substitution is only necessary when the outcome of the game becomes important. This only becomes relevant for the older age groups (11 or 12 years old).

- The importance of the result should be clearly emphasized in the older age groups (14 to 18 year olds). The strongest team should therefore be fielded when necessary.

- If a player in the A or B team is substituted, this should always be for a specific reason related to improving the team's play. After the game the coach should always explain this reason and analyze whether or not the switch worked ("the perfect substitution").

- Everyone must be made fully aware of how the team is expected to achieve a good result (during training sessions, coaching, team talks). In this way the players will begin to understand the coach's actions.

- For teams/players/age groups where results are less important, substitutions are made on a basis of everyone taking their turn.

Captaincy

- In the youngest age groups this role can perhaps be given to the group loud mouth, in the hope that he will be forced to look beyond his own feelings and emotions.

- In the older age groups the coach should encourage the captain to regulate various tasks within the group, so that the coach can continue to exert his influence on the field through the captain.

- When results start to matter (12-year-olds and upwards), it is in everyone's interest that the captain exerts a positive influence on the result.

- A player should not experience the captaincy as a burden, or have to do things against his will. Joint agreement should be sought on a player whose captaincy will enhance the team's performance.

- Often the group will contain a natural leader, so the coach must be sure to observe the group carefully.

Team selection

- Team selection involves thinking about how the available resources can best be deployed.

- Bearing in mind the development of his players' skills, a coach must always try to confront his best players with an element of challenge. There must be incentives to encourage players to adapt their game. For example, the B team's dominant sweeper could be transferred to a position in the A team's midfield.

- The line-up must reflect a vision of how youth soccer should be played. Choices must be made and justified to management, players, club officials, etc.

- Only in the oldest age group should the opposition's strengths be a factor in selecting the team, and even then it must not represent a break with the club's youth soccer concept (club style and philosophy, concept of the chief coach, etc.).

- Play the best players in positions where they can improve their game, i.e. the interests of a particular youth side in a certain competition must not be put first.

In certain circumstances a coach has to field his strongest team.

Coaching youngsters at different levels of development

Coaching is an aid to learning. Together with frequent practice, soccer coaching is an important tool for developing technical skills and teaching players to use these skills in competitive games. The end product of coaching should be enjoyment, mastery of the game and, of course, winning.

Coaching is an aid to learning.

There is one basic golden rule. Coaching is not about technique; coaching is about the game and how it unfolds, and about developing the players' proficiency and competitive maturity, and it is about enjoyment. However, there is still a lot of resistance to this point of view. Too much attention is paid to practicing individuals' technical skills in isolation, e.g. dribbling, feinting, controlling the ball, passing, etc. The technical skills which are necessary for playing soccer are too often developed as tricks, unrelated to the game or even the simplest situations.

We might equate this style of coaching to teaching someone how to swim on dry land; the most essential ingredient - water - is missing! The soccer equivalent of the water is the elements which serve to make up the game, i.e. the uses to which the players put their technique - in short, the purpose the players impose on the game.

Proficiency

Children used to develop their proficiency by playing in the streets or on the beach or in the gym. The games they played gave purpose to what they did: they played to win, and in order to win they developed their technique and their insight into the game. They certainly did not rely on a coach to tell them what to do.

In today's world most children no longer play on the street. Soccer has to be learned in a far shorter time, with the aid of a coach who has learned how to use small sided games to develop children's soccer proficiency. Initially basic games (e.g. 4 v 4, 1 v 1, 5 v 2, line soccer and positional games with goals) are used, while at a later stage all sorts of more complex games and competitive games are introduced to promote the players' progress. This is the most natural form of development and therefore the quickest.

Small sided and competitive games create an environment in which children are fully motivated and practice enthusiastically by playing. Young and old alike enjoy small sided games as part of their training sessions. The idea that serious training sessions are incompatible with enjoyment is outdated.

The best results are obtained by making training sessions as enjoyable as possible!

Obviously youngsters need certain basic skills in order to play soccer. But that is at far as it goes. These skills can be practiced within the framework of small sided games with clearly defined objectives.

For example we talk about practicing "aiming" rather than "passing". But even at this early stage it is important for children to use a pass in order to win.

The role of coaching

The time consuming method of learning by "trial and error" (i.e. trying things out and learning from your mistakes) must be compensated for by efficient training. This saves time.

There are a number of ways in which a coach can advance his players' development. These include:

- league games
- friendly games
- small sided games during training sessions
- small sided competitive games during training sessions
- practice drills during coaching sessions

The coach said "Stay on your feet as long as possible".

The coach's objectives

In view of a child's various stages of development, a coach clearly has a number of different objectives. Coaching for competitive matches should not begin until children reach the age of 12. There can be no doubt that children enjoy weekly matches, but the value of the complex competitive match in the learning process of young children must be put into its right perspective. A 7 v 7 game in one half of a normal-sized pitch is too complicated to be grasped properly by a group of 5 to 8 year olds. There are too many players involved and the field of play is too big. There is therefore increasing support for playing 4 v 4 instead of 7 v 7 at this age.

The older the children become, the better they are able to comprehend abstract terms such as length, speed, etc. As children grow older they are also better able to project their thoughts back or forward in time, i.e. they can form a picture of what is going to happen next or what has just happened. Children develop this facility when they are about age 12. Younger children have to be coached at the moment when a situation arises. It is pointless to refer back to the situation at half time, unless the coach can illustrate it visually in some other way. He might do this by, for example, demonstrating an error in technique and then showing how it can be corrected.

Because very young children are at a sensitive age and tend not to think beyond the immediate moment, coaching should be focused on developing their physical coordination and their technique. Insight and communication will play an important role at a later stage.

The development of soccer proficiency can be divided into four stages:

Preliminary stage (5 to 7 year olds)

The objective in the preliminary stage is simple: "Learning to control the ball".

The emphasis at this stage is on playing all kinds of soccer games. There is a certain level of organization however. Just giving each child a ball is not enough. Simplifying the game to its most elementary forms does not mean "forgetting" obstacles but rather setting them at a lower level. In the context of each game the children must clearly understand each of the following aspects:

- What is the point of this game? (What do we have to do, and how do I score points?)

- What direction is the game played in? (Always from point A to point B, and never in all possible directions or with goals on all sides of the playing area.)

- Each child must get to touch the ball as often as possible.

- Children should never be pressured to move in a specific way (children are not puppets!). Do suggest possible solutions or techniques they could use.

- Play 2 v 2, 3 v 3 and 4 v 4. Games with larger numbers are not suited to this age group.

It must resemble soccer.

The "city game" described on page 93, is a good model for this age group. Together with the information given above, it challenges coaches to be creative in devising games and developing new ideas.

Stage I: Developing basic proficiency (12 years old)

The aims are twofold
1. To use basic games to develop basic skills in a suitably simulated soccer environment.

2. To create an atmosphere of enjoyment and excitement in which children can become familiar with the different elements of the game and its difficulty factors (the obstacles and various ingredients of the game) such as three-dimensional awareness (height, length, depth), speed of action (time element), teammates, opposition, pressure, positional play, etc.

Precisely this interplay between physical and mental factors (the confrontation with genuine soccer obstacles) promotes the development of children's soccer proficiency. The basic games are described in more detail in Chapter 6.

Youngsters are usually ready for match-related coaching in development stages II and III. In practice however the different stages overlap.

Stage II: Developing competitive (11 v 11) proficiency (12 to 16 year olds)

At this stage the objective is firstly to extend the coaching objectives of stage I. The coach increases the difficulty factors by introducing more complex soccer obstacles. In this context it is also part of the coach's task to place very talented youngsters in a higher age group if he thinks they are up to it. A second objective at this stage is to develop an understanding of the tasks of the team, the tasks of each line of the team, and the tasks of each member of the team.

During training sessions the coach will use small sided and large sided competitive games (and derived forms) for this purpose.

If a coach is to help players to progress at this stage of their soccer development, he must have a knowledge of the tasks and functions of the team and its component parts. These are dealt with in Chapter 11.

Stage III: Developing team proficiency (16 to 18 years old)

The aim at this stage is to improve the productivity of the players. Team skills become apparent and are exploited. The team systematically follows specific objectives. The sum total of all the available skills in a team starts to contribute towards better team organization. Attention is paid to improving performance: "What must we do now to ensure that we win the championship?" All sorts of mental aspects begin to play a role. Players have to learn that it is sometimes better to hold back than to chase towards the ball. Many players will find themselves playing in the shadow of one or two "playmakers", because their positional tasks are more rigidly circumscribed. Their freedom to roam is curtailed by their task and function.

This represents the final stage of development towards "adult soccer".

At this stage the coach's most important task is to get the team to function as a cohesive unit: in defense, buildup and attack; whether in possession or trying to regain possession. The team must be able to overcome the opposition's resistance, and adjust flexibly to the state of the game and its ever changing pressures.

This means creating a unit which is capable of functioning with a determination to win matches, to score goals and avoid conceding them, to create goalscoring chances but deny them to its opponents. All in all a very complex task.

Tasks and team organization are important at this age.

COACHING OBJECTIVES

AGE	OBJECTIVES	CONTENT

5 - 7 year olds (preliminary stage)	• Feel for the ball
	
	• Ball control
	
	• "The ball and me"
		T.I.c.
		
		• Skill-oriented games
		  • Direction
		  • Speed
		  • Precision

7 - 12 year olds	• Basic proficiency	T.I.c. • Developing insight and technique by playing games involving simplified soccer situations (so-called basic games)
12 - 16 year olds	• Competitive proficiency (11 v 11)	T.I.C. • Teamwork, development of tasks per line and position through small sided and large sided competitive games (and derived forms of these games)

16 - 18 year olds	• Team proficiency	T.I.C.
		
		• Match Coaching
		  • Productivity Competitive proficiency
		  • Mental aspects

18 years old	• Proficiency at the top level	T.I.C. • Specialization or multifunctionality

T.I.C. = Technique - Insight - Communication
T.I.C. is based on observation

CHAPTER 5

READING THE GAME

The coach must have a good eye.

Before he starts a training session, a coach must think carefully about what he wants to achieve. Essentially he wants to improve the soccer performance of his players. Performance can best be analyzed under match conditions, where players are confronted with a wide range of difficult situations. The coach must have an eye for these situations. He must be able to isolate the soccer problems which arise, and he must then consider how he can deal with them in the next training session.

For new coaches an 11 v 11 match contains so many different incidents that it is almost impossible to abstract the most important shortcomings (soccer problems). It is therefore easier to read a game in which fewer players participate. Games of 4 v 4 are suitable for this purpose, especially in the case of the younger players, but games of 6 v 6 or 7 v 7 also offer the trainer sufficient opportunity to identify soccer problems. Such games can also be played during training sessions.

Soccer know-how and insight

In small sided games, soccer problems become much clearer for both the coach and his players. A simple aid to reading the game is to subdivide it into 3 main situations:

The three main soccer situations are:

1. Own team has possession.

2. Opposition has possession.

3. Change of possession: the moment when the ball is lost or won.

Players must be aware of what they have to do in each of these three situations. A number of general principles apply to each of them and can serve as guidelines for the players. We will deal with the three main situations within the following structure.

- **Meaning of the game!**
  What is our objective?

- **General principles**
  Tools to realize the meaning of the game. (How?)

1. Possession

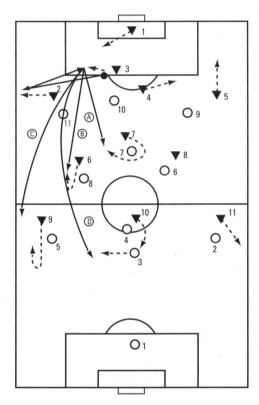

Game plan

- Move the ball down field in order to create chances (build up)

- Score goals

General principles

- Create as much space as possible
  - Width
  - Depth

- Aim to get forward; play the ball deep when possible

- Retain the ball (important precondition for achieving the objective of the game)

- Principle: playing the ball square paves the way for a forward pass.

- The team should try to maintain a good formation.

2. Opponents in possession

Game plan

- Disrupt the build up of the opposition

- Win the ball back

- Avoid conceding goals

General principles

- Make the field of play as small as possible, depending on the strength of the opposition:
  - Move towards the ball (pressing).
  - Move towards own goal (fall back).
  - Push towards the touchline (squeezing).

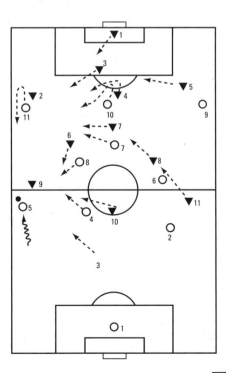

- Pressure the player who has the ball.

- Mark closely in the vicinity of the ball.

- Positional/zonal marking further away from the ball.

- Remain useful for as long as possible!

The team's game plan will not be achieved if a foul is committed, so avoid conceding free kicks.

Change of possession: the moment when the ball is lost or won.

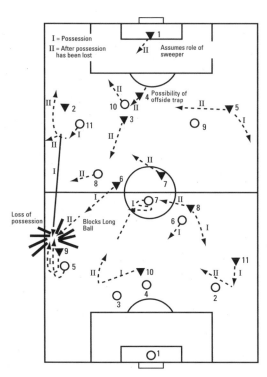

Game plan

- Switch game plan from "possession" to "opponents in possession" (or vice versa) as quickly as possible.

General principles

- **Loss of possession**
  - The player who is nearest the ball

attempts to stop it being played forward by pressurizing the player on the ball, so that he will play it square, hold it, run with it, play it back, etc.

- All players switch to making a contribution towards preventing a goal being scored, by: "squeezing" the opposing players
  (cutting off the options for moving inside)
  - blocking opponent's shot

  - choosing a position which will diminish any direct threat "pressing"

  - marking tight close to the ball if enough teammates are available "delaying"

  - positional/zonal marking if not enough teammates are available (delaying, not "diving in", not being passed).

Pressurizing the player in possession (without conceding a free kick)

• Winning the ball

- The player who gains possession (by intercepting a pass, winning a tackle, etc.) first looks to play it forward.

- The players further away from the ball "ask" for the ball (e.g. while hanging back to avoid the offside trap).

- The player who gains possession can also push the ball forward into space and run onto it himself in order to escape the offside trap (depending on where he is).

- Spread out to create as much space as possible.

- Try to stay out of your opponents' field of vision.

- Teammates of the player with the ball must take initiatives by anticipating where the ball will go, making dummy runs to draw attention away from teammates, etc.).

A long pass must be hit cleanly.

From buildup to attack

(In other words, how to get from your own to your opponents' penalty area).

> ## The quickest way is the long ball (e.g. Irish national team)

Preconditions:
- Requires good kicking technique (speed, height, direction).

- The ball must be "neutral", i.e. the player on the ball must have the time and space to make the pass (difficult with opponents nearby).

- An attacker must be able to receive the ball.

- There must be some degree of communication between the passer and the "receiver".

- Attacker must be able to recognize the instant when the deep ball can be played.

Positional play in order to be able to play a long ball forward

Preconditions:
- Requires insight into the purpose of positional play (what do we want to do?)

- Take up positions relative to the opposing players and the available space in such a way as to create situations when the longball can be played. Whether it will actually be played depends largely on whether a teammate moves into the right position at the right moment (ability of teammates to "read" the situation).

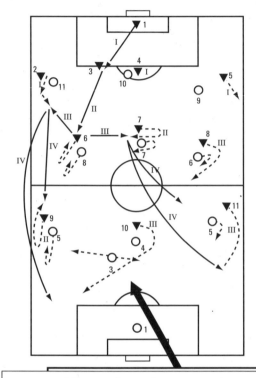

GOALKEEPER ROLLS THE BALL OUT TO 3; AT THE SAME TIME 4, 2, 5 AND 6 TAKE UP POSITION IN ORDER TO A) CREATE SPACE FOR THEMSELVES, B) GET OUT OF THE OPPONENT'S FIELD OF VISION AND C) MAKE SPACE FOR 3. 3 PASSES TO 6, WHILE 2, 7, 4 AND 5 TAKE UP NEW POSITIONS. 6 LAYS THE BALL OFF TO 7 OR 2, WHILE 8, 10, 9 AND 11 TAKE UP NEW POSITIONS.

The time won by playing the ball square or wide must be used to set up the deep pass!

- The quality of positional play can be improved by:
  - Moving the ball around faster (opponents have to run more).
  - Taking up position at the right moment (neither too soon nor too late).
  - Taking up the right position (not too close, not too far away).

From attack to defense after losing possession

In other words, what measures must be taken to ensure that a goal is not conceded, and the ball can be won back after possession is lost?

General principles

- As a first measure, the player who is nearest to the ball must employ every

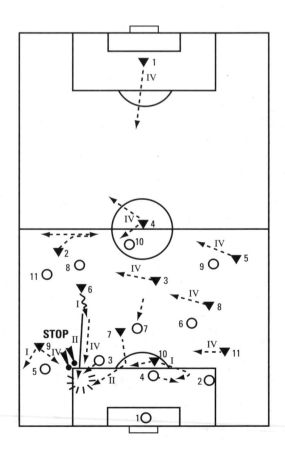

means to prevent the opposition playing a long ball forward. This might be the player who has just lost the ball, but often this player has overrun the point where the play broke down, so another player must take action.

- in the diagram, on page 31: 7 is beyond the ball, so 6 challenges the opponent 3 in possession.

- All players must immediately switch to "defensive mode"; - there is no time to indulge in emotions such as disappointment at losing the ball, etc. Players close to the ball must mark tightly. Further away from the ball the players must close down space, cover their teammates, mark zonally, etc. (see players 5, 8, and 11).

- The sweeper must decide whether to push up and play the offside trap or fall back and deprive the striker of space (4 in relation to the striker). If a number of strikers are involved the offside trap is more risky, more difficult to judge, and requires more communication and cooperation.

- The goalkeeper can act as an additional sweeper by advancing out of his penalty area.

- If there are too few players in the vicinity of the ball (e.g. they have been caught in attacking positions), the players on hand must carefully take up zonal covering positions and then attempt to delay their opponents by good positional play and by pressing up towards the ball, so that their team mates can get back into useful positions.

- When a team is on the attack, there

should always be a balance between the number of players actively involved in the attack and the number of players holding back to "lock the door" if possession is lost.

- Again the general principle is: deny the opposition space to play (push up towards the ball, be ready to spring the offside trap, close down space, and above all don't be passed -> remain useful for as long as possible).

The coach gives instructions.

ANALYZING SOCCER

SOCCER

↓

3 main moments in possession/ opponents in possession/transition

↓

meaning of the game

↓

tasks/functions described in space/time

↓

demands regarding T.I.C.

Technique
Insight ← Communication

CHAPTER 6

SOCCER TRAINING: A QUESTION OF PLAYING

Principles of the Dutch Soccer Association's concept

The Dutch Soccer Association's youth soccer concept is the result of observing and assessing the game at the youth level. It's main principles are set out below:

1. Getting the most out of the game

The more enthusiasm the players show for the game, the more they will get out of it, and the more they will learn. Youngsters will experience the game to the full if they get the feeling that they are really playing soccer. In days gone by, getting children interested in a knock-about on the streets was no problem at all. Kids would play for hours on end, day in, day out.

2. Lots of repetition

'Practice makes perfect' - children used to learn their soccer skills in the streets on the basis of this principle. The same game over and over again. The principle also applies to many other walks of life - if at first you don't succeed, try and try again. This is why soccer coaching needs little more than a few types of practice drills in which all the elements of soccer are present: a ball, a field of play with a certain size, goals, teammates, opponents and, last but not least, the rules of the game. By constantly repeating these practice drills, the players will be able to master the game much quicker than when they practice all kinds of different exercises which do not contain the ingredients of the game.

If we don't get started soon, we're not going to learn anything!

3. The right coaching

Unlike street soccer, an adult is always on hand at a soccer club. Training sessions and matches are played out under the supervision of team managers and coaches. Things aren't always as they should be. Players often fail to understand the remarks and instructions directed at them. The language used may be adult, properly suited for adult soccer but bearing little relationship to youth soccer. It is therefore important for coaches to understand exactly how youngsters experience the game, so that they can convey their message in a way which the players understand and act upon. A coach must also be capable of organizing training sessions and matches which satisfy the first two principles of the Dutch Soccer Association's concept. This means that coaches must be able to use soccer drills which get the most out of the players, and can be used again and again. Coaching is all about influencing soccer performance, and a coach must get his players to cope with solving soccer problems, and consequently their performance will improve.

Learning the game by playing it!

The Dutch Soccer Association's concept is a method of encouraging the soccer learning process in youngsters. We are convinced that it helps youngsters to become better soccer players and to enjoy playing soccer more.

Soccer players show their true colors in actual play. Their play demonstrates what they are really capable of, and reveals aspects of the game which they have not yet mastered. It also reflects their insight into soccer objectives.

Players' performances during a game guide the coach in his choice of training activities and his comments to them. A coach may have to point out to one player that, for example, when he attempts to beat an opposing player he starts to accelerate or feint too soon, i.e. too far away from his opponent. A second player might have to be coached in taking up a better position in relation to the opposing players, so that he and his teammates can control the situation more effectively. A third player may need some advice on how to pass the ball in such a way that the receiver can control it more easily.

Learn to control the ball first: make the ball do what you want it to.

It is impossible to formulate exact written instructions on how to help players to improve their game. A coach must be competent at reading (i.e. analyzing) the range of different situations which crop up in the game. Good soccer coaching demands an enormous amount of insight on the part of the coach, as well as the ability to interpret correctly the shortcomings and/or talents of his players and to involve the players in the search for solutions to the problems encountered.

THE DUTCH SOCCER ASSOCIATION'S CONCEPT

Elements every training session must include
Below is a point-by-point summary of the requirements each training session should satisfy.
Each training session can be analyzed using this checklist.

1. Typical Soccer Objectives	• Scoring/Preventing Goals • Buildup/Teamwork • Goal-Orientedness • Rapid Switch when change of Possession occurs
2. Many Repetitions	• Frequent Involvement • Short Waiting Times • Good Planning/Organization • Sufficient Balls/Equipment **Playing to Win!**
3. Group Considerations	• Age • Ability • Perception (serious of casual) **Pay Attention to Work-Rest Ratio!**
4. Correct Coaching (Influence)	• Make Objectives Clear • Influence and Teach Players By: Intervening/Stopping Play, Giving Instructions, Asking Questions, Encouraging Suggestions, Setting an Example, Demonstrating.

1 + 2 + 3 + 4 = IDEAL CLIMATE FOR LEARNING

How to improve players' performances

Coaching helps to improve players' knowledge and insight into the game. Coaching is all about improving players' performances, and players' performances can best be analyzed under match conditions. A match will contain a whole range of incidents which present problems for players.

A coach must have an understanding of such situations and be able to identify soccer problems which arise during a match. After the match, the coach should formulate his objectives for the next training session and consider how he can best achieve them.

A coach can simplify the soccer teaching process by going through a number of steps when he analyzes the game. This will facilitate the coaching of youngsters.

Step 1
Observation in relation to the three main phases of the game.

1. When own team has possession.

2. When the opposition has possession.

3. When possession changes, i.e. the ball is won or lost.

Step 2
Simplification of the 11 v 11 format to a (more) manageable level, e.g. 4 v 4 or 5 v 5.

Step 3
A coach must ensure that the soccer problems he identifies also become the concern of his players. The coach must teach his players to choose better, more effective options. The players' contributions to the team effort must be improved.

Players must not play better just because the coach tells them to do so, but because the soccer situation demands it of them. Depending on the standard of play, the coach must be able to take measures during training sessions which will accentuate a given problem. This is the most essential aspect of a coach's task, i.e. his ability to manipulate typical soccer obstacles and difficulty factors for the purpose of improving his players' performance.

Soccer obstacles:

- **The ball** (already discussed)

- **Opposing players** (the more opponents and the better their play, the more difficult soccer becomes).

- **Teammates** (players must be able to work together and must know their positions and responsibilities - this takes time and patience)

- **The rules of the game** (playing or practicing with or without certain rules influences the way in which the game is played, e.g. with or without the offside rule).

- **Goal-orientedness** (soccer is not played in just any direction but from goal to goal within a measured area; the players must therefore play in a certain direction).

- **Stress** (a player may succeed in everything he does during a training session, but might fail in a real match in front of a crowd, cameras, the press, etc.).

- **Time** (the more time a player has, the easier it is to play; playing soccer against lesser opposition is therefore less demanding).

- **Space** (a team will usually find it easier to retain possession in its own half than in its opponents' penalty area).

The coach can also introduce elements such as the following:
A. Objectives, e.g.:
- A goal has to be scored.
- The opposition has to be prevented from scoring.

- Wait until opponents make an error.
- A few minutes more and the game will be won.

B. Time, e.g.:
Speed:
- A goal has to be scored as quickly as possible.
- The ball has to be retained as long as possible.

Situation:
- The ball is won.
- Throw-in/switch the play.

C. Space, e.g.:
- Position close to opponents' goal.
- In team's own penalty area.
- In team's own half.

D. Function, e.g.:
Roles:
- Finisher.
- Goalkeeper.
- Playmaker.

Responsibilities:
- Outside right.
- Left back.

The ball is the biggest obstacle for beginners.

Step 4

The ability to read the game within simplifications of 11 v 11 (looking at one of the main phases of the game, reducing the number of players, taking account of the obstacles). The coach should make detailed notes of everything which catches his eye.

He makes comments on what the players do. These comments come under different headings, e.g.:

- Technical:
  pace of the ball, ball played to the correct foot, how the ball is played and received.

- Insight:
  too impatient, not direct enough, too lazy, too greedy, tends to dive in, concedes unnecessary free-kicks (= loss of possession).

- Communication
  misunderstandings such as playing a long ball into space instead of to the striker's feet.

Beating a tackle.

Step 5

The coach must take the right steps in the right order if he is to influence the way his charges play.

The coach must manipulate the obstacles (difficulty factors).

We call this methodology!

Examples:

- Increase or decrease the number of players.

- Let numerically unequal teams play against each other (e.g. 6 v 5, 4 v 3, 3 v 2).

- Give players specific tasks.

- Modify the size (i.e. length, width) of the playing area.

- Play with or without goals, or with several goals (on the goal line).

- Modify the rules, or make a rule inapplicable.

- Ask the players to achieve an objective within a limited time (e.g. score a goal within a minute)

Examples of how obstacles can be manipulated in a small sided game of 4 v 4 (as a simplification of the 11 v 11 match format) are discussed in detail in Chapter 8. The organization and the players' tasks in a specific drill must be clearly understood by players and coach alike, as must the objectives.

The translation of the practice drill into a real match situation (11 v 11) is vital.

Step 6

The coach must repeatedly refer to comparative situations in actual matches. The obstacles in the training drills can be compared with situations which occur in real matches. The coach will also want to discuss a number of specific obstacles observed in the match.

These might be:

- Communication between players and lines
- Rules of the game
- Result/importance of the game
- The team's formation and that of the opposition
- Specific abilities/shortcomings of the team's players (specialists in heading, passing, defending, shooting, running) and the opposition.
- Positional play when in possession and when the opposition has possession.

Formulating soccer problems

In order to get coaching results, soccer problems must first be clearly formulated (in other words, what exactly is going wrong?).

Important elements of the problem description are:

A. What is going wrong with regard to the soccer objectives?

B. Who are the key players - what are their positions?

C. When does the problem arise?

D. In which area of the pitch does the problem arise?

E. Are other specific aspects involved which are related to the players or the circumstances? (Importance of the game, position in league table, weather, state of the pitch, etc.)

The players themselves must be able to identify the problem and accept that solving it comes down to them. Obviously more can be expected of the older age groups than of the youngest children.

Examples

A. We rarely create scoring opportunities.

B. The quality of the long balls played up to the attackers is very poor.

C. The rapport between the players building up and attackers is poor - they don't understand each other.

D. During buildup play in the team's own half, the defenders are not able to create the space they need to play a long ball.

E. This problem is exacerbated when the opposing strikers put pressure on the defenders.

Identifying objectives

Once the problem has been identified, objectives must be set for the next training session.

Setting objectives

The objectives should be formulated on the basis of:

A problem which has been identified is always a soccer problem, so... analyze the game.

Define the problem as precisely as possible, in terms of:

- Time
- Space
- Function

General objectives can also be specified per age group (see stages of soccer proficiency on page 28).

For example:

When the team wins the ball and starts its buildup play in defense, the defenders need so much time on the ball that they have few opportunities to play a long pass, despite the fact that their strikers take up good positions.

Concentrating on her task.

Examples

A number of very common but widely varied soccer problems are detailed below.

- Lack of understanding of the game (the players don't understand the intention, the solution and the execution).

- Technical execution in certain situations (the players may know what to do in a given situation but lack the technical skills needed to put their knowledge into practice).

- Physical aspects (the players are not able to cope at a particular level, certain players continue to show deficiencies in a specific position).

- Mental aspects (players give up when they are required to chase after the ball for long periods, or lose their composure when something goes wrong or the referee makes a bad decision). Incidentally all soccer problems are to a greater or lesser extent in the mind.

In order to set up a training situation properly, a knowledge and understanding of all problem areas is essential.

However... this knowledge should never be seen in isolation, but always in relation to the actual game.

Some forms of soccer conditioning, for example, are too often derived from theories of exercise physiology.

More is needed than a knowledge of exercise physiology.

Soccer training is conditioning and conditioning is soccer training. Insights gained from exercise physiology need to be translated into exercises which are suitable for soccer players.

Know-how relating to:
- exercise and physical capacity
- ways of exercising
- methodology of exercise
- control over the exercise

must be translated into soccer terms by the coach (see Chapter 10).

> **There is no single answer to the question of how to coach.**

To summarize, soccer training means the following:

The more soccer experience, coaching experience, soccer know-how, knowledge of youth soccer, and soccer teaching expertise a coach possesses, the better he will be able to solve soccer problems and the less likely he will be to resort to drills and practice material which seem to be soccer-related but in reality ignore the main problems.

Coaches must be able to:

- Formulate soccer problems: who, what and where?

- Convince players that the problem is not the "coaches problem", but a "players' problem".

- Read the game.

Learning soccer/learning coaching

Observation: Reading the game, watching soccer in relation to the three main situations.
1. Possession
2. Possession by the opposition
3. The transition from 1 to 2 (losing possession) and from 2 to 1 (gaining possession)

Starting situation: Age - ability level - perception

Analysis: Formulating soccer problems

Objectives: Taking into account: age - ability level - motivation

Realization: Practical coaching:
- Organization
- Choice of practice drills
- Exercise and physical capacity
- Level of influence

Evaluation: Has the objective been achieved? (Tie in with all other steps involved).

Coaching Plan for Youth Soccer

Warming up

A training session is usually preceded by a warming up period which is intended to get the players properly primed for a spell of vigorous exertion.

After warming up the players must be fully concentrated and the muscles must be able to cope with sudden stresses (e.g. sprinting, stopping suddenly; in all kinds of different directions and against opposition from other players).

The warming up period should be able to hold the youngsters' interest and, especially in the case of the youngest players, it should be light-hearted. An atmosphere needs to be generated which builds up players' enthusiasm.

This seems easy when you have short legs.

Warming up should be carried out as much as possible with the ball, i.e. do not start with laps of the pitch "to get warm". The players must be familiar with the exercises chosen by the coach and they must be able to perform them easily. Warming up has a different objective for the youngest players than for the older ones, and is therefore carried out differently.

Warming up for beginners

For the youngest players the main objectives of the warming up period are to create the right mood, to let the players blow off steam, and to get them to listen to the coach.

Options:

- Give each player a ball. Players take it in turn to run from the halfway line towards the goal with the ball at their feet:
  - Play the ball along the ground or through the air into the goalkeeper's hands (he has to warm up too).
  - Try to score a goal with a shot along the ground.
  - Try to score a goal with a shot through the air.

  The players should stay on the move as much as possible. Make sure there is enough space to run with the ball, etc.

- Many games are suitable for the youngest age groups (where each player has a ball).
  One example is the "city game". Players develop technical skills without realizing it.

- One ball between two players: play the ball back and forth towards the goal (play the ball into the goalkeeper's hands, etc.)

Warming up for juniors (12 - 17 years)

The importance of the warming up session is greater for juniors. Players grow faster at this age, and in many cases the development of muscle tissue can hardly keep pace with the growth of bones.

A lot is demanded of the muscles, not least because more is now asked of the players. Ideally the coach should be able to persuade his players that warming up is essential and to explain how this can best be done.

Juniors can of course do warming up exercises on their own, just as they do before matches. This saves time during the training session. Start off slowly and then raise the tempo.

Stretching exercises may follow a reasonable amount of exercise (good blood circulation in the muscles).

Concentration is required even when stretching muscles.

If you don't succeed in getting players to do their own warming up exercises, we advise that you try using some practice drills involving use of a ball.

Options

- The same drills used by beginners, e.g. playing the ball in tandem towards the goals:
  - Play the ball into the goalkeeper's hands.
  - Along the ground or in the air.
  - Try to score with a shot along the ground.
  - Try to score with a shot through the air.

NB: Allow sufficient space between each pair of players, so they do not get in each other's way (run back via the touchlines). Players must stay on the move as much as possible.

- Play familiar positional games, e.g. 2 v 1, 3 v 1, 4 v 1, 4 v 2, 5 v 2, 6 v 2, etc.

  Constant coaching is not required in these situations. The games can be played in an open space or an area which has been coned off.

  If the ball is intercepted by a defender, swap roles (defender-attacker). Play for a period of one minute, then take a break. Use this break (e.g. one minute) for making brief observations, and keep the players busy by getting each pair to per form simple drills (keeping the ball in the air, heading, etc.)

- Use small sided games such as 4 v 4, 3 v 3, or 2 v 2 as a preliminary exercise, with real goals and lines (line soccer).

Stretching exercises are often used in training sessions. These are useful once adolescent growth starts, i.e. from the age of 13. For players who grow rapidly, this becomes even more important.

You should only ask the players to carry out stretching exercises if you are familiar with how the most important muscle groups have to be stretched (calf, thigh and groin muscles). The warming up period can be concluded with a drill which will stimulate the players for the rest of the training session (e.g. a competitive small sided game).

Finally it should be noted that, for older age groups, the warming up session is a means of emphasizing that the team must work together to achieve its objective (i.e. winning a match).

Some of the warming up should be done collectively (to get players into the right frame of mind for a match or training session).

Cooling down

At the end of a training session, balls and other accessories often have to be tidied away and there may be a short discussion. Both these activities are important. The players are also responsible for treating equipment with respect and putting it away.

It is important to keep the players' attention, for example to discuss the next match or to get some feedback on what they thought of the training session. After a strenuous training session some time must be devoted to cooling down, with light stretching and running exercises.

Even professionals have to be supervised during warming up.

Warming up and cooling down

Spend about 20 minutes on warming up exercises before each match/training session (with the whole team across the width of the pitch).

1. Limbering up
(approx. 5 minutes)

- Running exercises and physical exercises such as swinging the arms, cross-steps, skipping, twisting the torso, lifting the

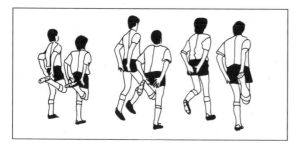

2. Stretching exercises
(approx. 7 minutes)

- Only start with stretching exercises after completing the limbering up exercises (sweat on forehead).

- Be sure to use the correct starting position (see diagrams).

- Stretch muscle until pain barrier is reached (without causing any pain!)

Remember: Hold the stretch, don't bounce!

 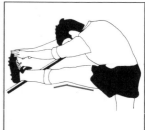

- Hold the stretch for 10 or 20 seconds.

- Repeat exercise on other side of body (repeat the whole exercise two to three times).

- Limbering exercises may be carried out in between, e.g. swinging the legs or arms.

3. Soccer exercises
(approx. 8 minutes)

- Soccer exercises, in order to give the players the feeling that a good soccer performance is going to be required of them.

- Several players pass the ball, run after the ball, varying direction, speed, distance, playing the ball along the ground and through the air. Positional play (e.g. 3 v 2 - familiarization with real soccer obstacles).

- Goalkeepers help each other to warm up (try not to beat the other keeper too often, as this could cause loss of self-confidence).

- Drink sufficient liquid after the warming up period, during intervals and after training sessions and matches, especially during tournaments (drink as much as possible between matches).

4. Match/training session

- Ensure that the time between the warming up period and the training session or match is kept to a minimum (optimal effect).

5. Cooling down
(approx. 10 minutes)

- Cooling down is the reverse of warming up, a combination of 2 and 1 (i.e. stretching and gentle running exercises).

- Cooling down exercises are also necessary between matches in a tournament as a form of preparation for the next game, which of course is preceded by warming up.

Basic games, competitive games and practice games

Use practice drills sparingly

Soccer coaching isn't about immersing players in all kinds of drills. Coaching means working effectively to improve soccer performance. To youngsters, playing soccer is all about mastering the fundamentals of the game and developing the necessary basic skills. The result of the game is secondary. For older players (above the age of 13), their performance is synonymous with getting the best possible game result; winning is then an important objective.

> The main purpose of a training session is to teach players. The learning process is characterized by repetition. As the players learn to recognize, deal with and recall certain recurrent situations (which are closely related to situations which occur in real matches), they find it easier to make the right decision in subsequent situations.

That is why an attempt has been made to devise a limited number of basic games which meet the requirements set out in the concept of the Dutch Soccer Association. All these games are characterized by their close relationship to "real" soccer, in that they focus on certain typical soccer problems and encourage the players to learn specific aspects of the game.

The motivational factors are present in the basic forms themselves. It is clear that a coach can draw on his know-how and insight to give added value to these games through the quality of his coaching.

Categories of different basic games associated with the main situations of soccer games, with associated practice games.

BUILDUP
(possession)

2	v 1
2	v 2
3	v 1
4	v 2
4	v 3 (see description)
3	v 2
3	v 3
5	v 2 (see description)
5	v 3
5	v 4
4	v 4
5	v 5

Focus on these players

- these games can be played as they stand, or additional obstacles can be introduced, e.g. one or more extra attackers to encourage attacking play.

- the players in possession and their opponents attempt to realize soccer objectives, i.e.:
  - creating scoring chances (buildup and attack)
  - preventing goals being scored
  - intercepting the ball (regaining the ball back and breaking out).

Teamwork is fundamental to soccer.

- These games emphasize the following aspects:

INSIGHT/ COMMUNICATION	TECHNICAL SKILLS
• running in space • asking for the ball • keeping at a distance • working together • creating space • switching the play • one-touch play	• passing • kicking • dribbling, pushing the ball forward • controlling the ball • (stopping, trapping, receiving, ect.) • beating a man • holding the ball

ATTACKING
(possession)

1	v 1 (see description)
1	v 2
2	v 1 (see description)
3	v 1
2	v 2
2	v 3
3	v 2 (see description)
3	v 3
3	v 4
4	v 2
4	v 3 (see description)
4	v 4
4	v 5
5	v 4

↑
Focus on these players

- These games should be played with the objective of scoring. The attackers try to score and the defenders try to prevent this and to switch to their own buildup and/or attack.

- Just as in a real match, goals are present. There may or may not be a goalkeeper. The objectives can be emphasized by replacing the goal with a line or a number of small goals.

- Specific objectives can also be realized by modifying the size of the playing area.

- As well as the aspects which fall under the heading of buildup, the following aspects are dealt with:

INSIGHT/ COMMUNICATION	TECHNICAL SKILLS
• scoring/finishing • creating chances	• shooting • passing • heading • dummying

DEFENDING
(opposition in possession)

1	v 1 (see description)
2	v 1 (see description)
3	v 1
3	v 2 (see description)
4	v 2
5	v 2
5	v 3
5	v 4
4	v 4 (see description)
5	v 5

↑
Focus on these players

- The following aspects are dealt with:

INSIGHT/ COMMUNICATION	TECHNICAL SKILLS
• protecting goal • provide cover • zonal marking • balancing the defense • taking over a mark • disrupting • forcing errors • chasing • delaying/gaining time • challenging for the ball	• winning the ball • man-to-man marking • slide tackle • block tackle • heading • fore-checking • 1 v 1 challenges • dummying on the ball

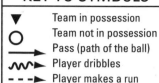

KEY TO SYMBOLS

▼	Team in possession
O	Team not in possession
→	Pass (path of the ball)
∿►	Player dribbles
- - -►	Player makes a run

Important: In all these games the first aspect is practicing certain elements within the context of one of the main situations in the game of soccer, such as "own team in possession" (attacking) or "opposition in possession" (defending). However, the moment at which the ball is won or lost (i.e. change in possession) is more important, and it must be recognized, used and capitalized on during the game.

Small sided and competitive small sided games:

The games described above can be categorized as practice games. They are very simplified manifestations of "real" matches in that:

A. A problem faced in a match is made clear (reinforced).

B. The players are frequently confronted with the problem
(many repetitions are possible).

C. The idea of playing soccer, the objectives of all those involved,

There are also a number of games and competitive games which more closely resemble real games, but differ from them in that the number of players, the size of the pitch and the rules can be modified. These forms encompass the three main moments in the game of soccer; "own team in possession", "opponents in possession" and "change of possession". However, coaching can also be focused on just one of these moments.

. . .and now go past him!

These games can also be played with lines instead of goals, so that the players have to dribble across the line to score, or with a number of smaller goals.

The nature of a game can also be changed by changing the size of the pitch. A long, narrow pitch (90 yards long x width of penalty area), for example, can be used to practice switching from buildup to attack (see diagram). The diagram represents an 8 v 8 game with two goalkeepers. The rules of the game, especially the offside rule, will have an important influence on the way the play develops (additional difficulty factor).

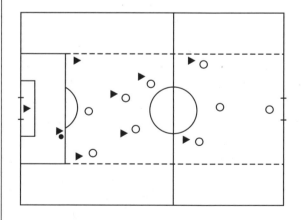

Games and competitive games can also be played in which one team has a numerical advantage, e.g. 6 v 5 or 8 v 7. This can be used to focus on a particular problem, e.g. if players are unable to get into scoring positions quickly enough, having an extra man can force them to use good positional play and move the ball around faster in order to get close to their opponents' goal more quickly.

The team with fewer players can be allowed to score by dribbling the ball across a line or by increasing the number of goals (see diagram).

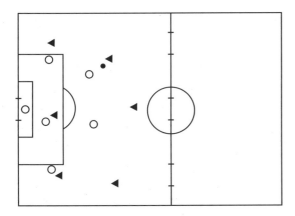

The most common games and competitive games are:

	Variations include:
6 v 6	6 v 5
7 v 7	7 v 6
8 v 8	8 v 7

The decision to use one or the other of these games depends largely on:

- the ability level of the players

- the perception of the players

- the age of the players

The choice of game should always be based on the need for players to perform as many soccer actions as possible within the available time:

- Get going as quickly as possible (e.g. "start with the 1st pass is free").

- Choose the correct soccer obstacles, e.g. number of opponents, pitch size, and appropriate task (competitive or practice game).

4 v 4 precedes the more advanced small sided and competitive games.

A few examples

How these examples are handled.

The main moments of the game of soccer are the starting point for describing a number of basic games in more detail. A number of games are discussed in the category "own team in possession".

A further subdivision is then made into "buildup" and "the attack". In the category "opposition in possession" a number of games are dealt with under the heading "defense".

The table illustrates this:

Please note:

Coaching can only be given in relation to one of the main moments of the game, if there is resistance from the opposing team.

If this resistance is inadequate, one of the coach's options is to coach the opposing team. For example, if a 5 v 2 game is being played and the 2 defenders do not pressure the ball, the attacking players are under no pressure, and have no incentive to put any effort into their positional play. In these circumstances the attackers have little need for coaching, so the coach can turn his attention to the defenders.

POSSESSION		OPPOSITION IN POSSESSION
Buildup	**Attack**	**Defense**

Buildup

	2	v 1
	2	v 2
	3	v 1
	4	v 2
A	4	v 3 (see description)
	3	v 2
B	3	v 3
	5	v 2 (see description)
	5	v 3
J	4	v 4 (see description)
	5	v 5

Attack

C	1	v 1 (see description)
	1	v 2
D	2	v 1 (see description)
	2	v 2
	2	v 3
E	3	v 2 (see description)
	3	v 3
	3	v 4
	4	v 3
J	4	v 4 (see description)
	4	v 5
	5	v 4
	5	v 5

Defense

F	1 v	1	(see description)
G	2 v	1	(see description)
	3 v	1	
H	3 v	2	(see description)
	4 v	2	
I	4 v	3	(see description)
	5 v	3	
	5 v	4	
J	4 v	4	(see description)
	5 v	5	

Focus on these players

The games described are listed in the above table. Each game is dealt with as follows:

1. Main moment (own team in possession, opposition in possession, change of possession)
2. Buildup, attack, defense
3. Purpose of the game (what needs to be learned?)
4. What the coach sees (observation and analysis)
5. What the coach does or says (instructions, methodology, organization)
6. Objective, organization and variations of the game depicted in diagram form.
7. Different options (other obstacles)
8. Organization in diagram form

The opponent's resistance determines the value of the exercise.

4 v 3 (see diagram A1) # A

Objective:

- for the 4 players to get past their 3 opponents, after which:
    1. they can score themselves (diagram A2)
    2. the ball can be played to the midfielders or attackers (diagram A3)

What the coach sees:	What the coach does/says:
1. The ball is lost quickly	1. Tells the players to keep possession of the ball, use their technique more effectively, slow the pace, improve their positional play and organization.
2. The opposing players are not beaten as quickly as they should be (ball persistently played square)	2. Tells the players to move the ball around faster, improve their passing and ball control, get into position quicker, be more direct, look for the right moment to play a long ball (or getting into an up field position).
3. Player in possession can only play the ball square or backwards (see diagram G2 4 v 3 with striker)	3. Tells the attackers (strikers) that they must read the positional play of their defenders and ask for a long pass at the right moment, i.e. when a teammate has the ball on his stronger foot and has enough time and space to play the pass.
4. 4-man team lacks vision, imagination and concentration needed to exploit the rare moments when a long ball can be played	4. Stresses to the strikers the importance of asking for the long ball at the right moment. Narrows the field of play to encourage defenders to play long balls (accentuates the problem).
5. Too few teammates available to receive a pass near the player in possession	5. Tells the teammates without the ball to take up better positions, "Keep some distance between each other", "Don't get in each other's way, create more space".

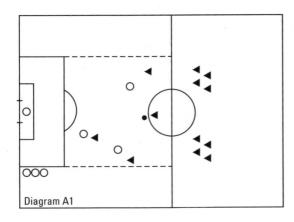

Diagram A1

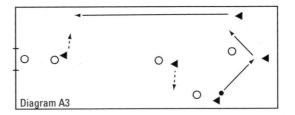

Diagram A3

Diagram A2:

- The 4 attackers attempt to get past 3 defenders and score a goal.
- The 3 defenders attempt to contain the attackers, to win the ball, and to 'score' by dribbling the ball across the line.

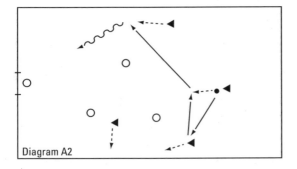

Diagram A2

Diagram A3:

From a 4 v 3 situation the ball is played up field to a striker and play continues with 5 v 4.

Play out the game, or continue until the attackers score a goal or the defenders dribble the ball across the line.

Organization of 4 v 3:

e.g. 3 teams of 4 players:
- Teams rotate after each turn
- 2 teams of 3 players who defend (when they win the ball they can score by dribbling the ball across the line)
- Always play in the same direction
- Allow players to change roles (attack - buildup - defense)
- Pay attention to work-rest ratio
- Modify field of play depending on the players' familiarity with the game and the coaching objectives (speed, accuracy, switching quickly, etc.)

Screening the ball when it has been won, is a technical ability.

POSSESSION
Buildup
5 v 2 (see diagram B2)

B

Objectives:
- Retaining possession (team play)
- Developing technical skills when confronted with soccer obstacles (space, time, opponents, goal-orientedness)
- Switching the play under pressure from a defender

KEY TO SYMBOLS	
▼	Team in possession
O	Team not in possession
──►	Pass (path of the ball)
⌒⌒⌒►	Player dribbles
- - -►	Player makes a run

What a coach sees:	What the coach does/says:
1. The ball is lost because: the players get too close to each other	1. "Create more space" "Keep some distance between yourselves, move apart" Increases the playing area so that the players have more space (move the cones)
2. the ball is played too quickly	2. "Keep hold of the ball, there are no opponents nearby"
3. the ball is held for too long	3. "Pass the ball sooner, don't let your opponent get close to the ball"
4. the pace and direction of the pass is not good	4. "Don't play the ball too gently, too hard, too high" "Don't play the ball too hard to a player who is sprinting into space" "Play the ball on the stronger foot, to the stronger side" "Make allowances for the surface (bumpy, wet)"
5. the players take up poor positions, fail to run into space, fail to work together	5. Playing area is too small, increase the size of the pitch (move cones). "Take up a position where you can receive a pass" "Use the space to full advantage" "Stop running under each other's feet" "Run into space" "Don't run in the same direction/line as your teammate" "Choose the right moment to let your teammates know exactly where you want the ball" "Don't all go for the ball" "Don't all hang back" "All five of you have to position yourselves to take full advantage of the available space" "Try to create more than just one option" "Vary long and short balls" "Try to move into space and ask for the long ball"
6. Possession is no longer lost.	6. Takes measures to make things more difficult for the 5-man team: • reduces the playing area by moving the cones • restricts the number of times the ball may be touched (e.g. 2-touch or 1-touch play) • coaches defenders • brings in an extra (3rd) defender

Organization:
Mark out 2 or 3 playing areas measuring 35 x 20 yards each or smaller, depending on the ability level of the players.

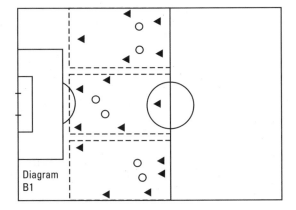

Diagram B1

Organization:

- Ensure that play flows: continuity is of the essence.
- Playing area is a rectangle, giving a directional aspect to the positional play.
- Size of playing area: this depends largely on the objectives; e.g. for beginners and less talented older players the area of play needs to be larger in order to keep the play flowing; players at this level need more time and space to keep the ball moving. The more skillful the players, the smaller the playing area can be. The norm is 35 - 20 yards. The area of play can also be modified by making it longer, or the play can be oriented towards a particular goal.
- Number of players: start with 5 attackers and 2 defenders. It has been found that this ratio is the most appropriate for achieving the objectives of this game (i.e. learning to play as a team/positional play). Depending on the ability level of the players and how they cope with the difficulty factors (time, space, opponents), some modifications may be needed, e.g. 3 defenders instead of 2. It is particularly advantageous to use goalkeepers in the role of defenders. If a larger field of play is

used (e.g. 55 - 30 yards), the same objectives can be attempted with a larger number of players. In such a situation the emphasis can be put on the long pass/crossfield pass/forward pass, etc. (e.g. 8 v 5 or 8 v 6).

- Role of defenders: two defenders should regularly be replaced - long periods of chasing aggressively after the ball take a lot out of the players. This is essential if the objective is to be achieved. If no defending takes place then the attackers have no incentive to demonstrate good positional play. It is therefore essential to bring in fresh defenders at frequent intervals and to incorporate sufficient rest periods.
- Competitive game/incentives
  The game can be made more attractive and the objectives can be emphasized by giving the game a competitive character, e.g.: for the 5 attackers:
  - 10 consecutive passes win one point
  - 10 one-touch passes win one point
  for the 2 defenders:
  - 1 interception (touching the ball) wins one point
  - 1 interception (winning the ball) wins one point
  - intercepting the ball and dribbling it out of the rectangle wins one point
  - intercepting the ball and scoring (with or without the aid of a teammate) in one or more goals wins one point.

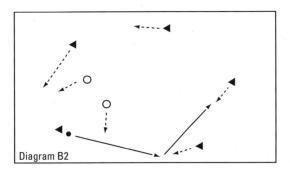

Diagram B2

POSSESSION
Attack
C

1 v 1 (see diagram C1)
Objective:

• Beating the opponent (must relate to real match situation as much as possible)

What a coach sees:	What the coach does/says:
1. The ball is lost before reaching the opponent 2. The player in possession cannot beat the defender 3. The player in possession beats the defender but doesn't know what to do 4. The attacker loses the ball (and therefore becomes the defender)	1. "Don't be so hasty, take your time" "Make sure that you have the ball under control" 2. "Don't kick the ball too far in front of you" "You are running too quickly/slowly" "You are not feinting" "You are feinting too soon" "Your feint is too obvious" "You are not accelerating as you go past your opponent" "Try learning how to feint before next week (homework)" 3. "Go for goal and score" "Cut across the defender" "Get the ball onto your shooting foot" 4. "Switch to defending as quickly as possible" "Try to get back" "Delay your opponent for as long as possible" "Stay on your feet as long as possible"

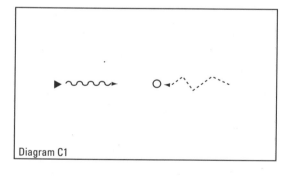

Diagram C1

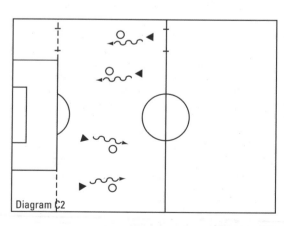

Diagram C2

Organization:

- The organization and approach depend on the objectives, the ability level of the players, and the age of the players.
- The main considerations are:
  - There must be lots of situations where players are beaten or avoid being beaten
  - The game must be rewarding for the players in terms of scoring goals, winning possession, etc.
  - There must be a relationship to "real" match situations
- 1 v 1 game of line soccer in marked-out playing area; 1 v 1 with goals (see diagram C2.); 1 v 1 with full-size goal + goalkeeper (see diagram C3.)
- Change the pairings so that the players do not always face the same opponent.

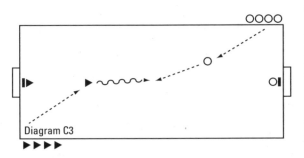

Diagram C3

Screen the ball when it has been won.

- Follow up 1 v 1 with:
  - attempt on goal
  - cross
  - pass
- After change of possession the roles switch immediately(a soccer skill)
- The player in possession should initially be given ample opportunity to score or dribble across the line
- The scoring opportunities should then be limited by shortening the line or making the goal smaller
- The work-rest ratio is important in this game. Fatigue has a negative effect on the execution of the move (inability to get past the defender, difficulty in switching from attack to defense, general lack of mobility); try a maximum of 30 - 60 seconds work and then 1 - 2 minutes active rest (e.g. practicing ball skills). The coach should watch out for signs of tiredness (shortage of breath, need to stop, lack of alertness, increased mistakes, etc.).

Try to cut off the pass.

POSSESSION
Attack
2 v 1 (see diagram D1)
Objective:
- For the 2 players to get past their opponent, after which:
    1. they can try to score
    2. the ball can be crossed

D

What a coach sees:	What the coach does/says:
1. The ball is passed around simply for the sake of it	1. If the defender takes up a bad position or marks the wrong man, you can go through to score yourself
2. The player in possession cannot get past the defender after passing the ball to his teammate	2. The 1-2 combination is initiated too far away from the defender, giving him time to recover The pass to the second player is too gentle (gives the defender more time) and therefore needs to be hit harder The pass to the second player is inaccurate or too hard, so time is lost in bringing the ball under control and there is no opportunity of playing a controlled first-time through ball back to the first player; make sure the pass is accurate
3. The player in possession loses the ball to the defender	3. "Don't let the defender to get too close" "Don't approach the defender too quickly" "Don't get too close to the defender" "Play the ball sooner" "The second player always runs into cover" "Don't push the ball too far in front of you, keep it under control"

4. The attackers beat the defender too easily	4. The playing area must be narrowed to encourage:
	    more individual runs
	    short 1-2 combinations
	    more takeovers
	The offside rule is introduced

5. The defender recovers after having been beaten	5. Once you have beaten the defender, go through as quickly as possible and score Cut across the defender's path if necessary Keep the ball in a good position for shooting
6. The second attacker hangs back once the defender has been beaten	6. "Keep up with your teammate - you might be needed to help take the ball past the goalkeeper"
7. The ball is lost and the defender has a chance of scoring (e.g. by dribbling the ball over the line)	7. "If you lose the ball, get back as quickly as possible. Incidentally, you shouldn't be able to lose the ball".

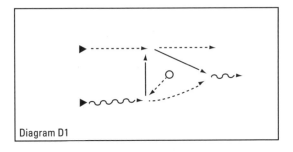

Diagram D1

The various options:

The two attackers can choose from a number of options, depending on the situation (own qualities and qualities of opponent).

1. If the defender goes to challenge the player in possession, a good option is to play a 1-2 combination (see diagram D2).

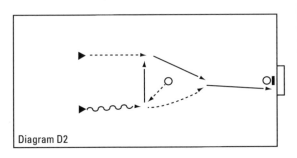

Diagram D2

2. If the defender backs off and concentrates on the attacker without the ball, the player in possession can go through on his own (see diagram D3).

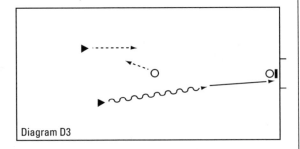

Diagram D3

3. If the defender covers the space behind him but does not challenge for the ball, the attacker who is not in possession can take the initiative by taking over the ball and sprinting past the defender (see diagram D4). The player in possession

could also take the initiative (e.g. a winger on the touch line who dribbles inside, creates space, then allows the ball to be taken over by a midfielder coming up outside of him).

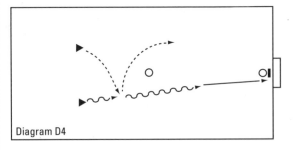

Diagram D4

Organization:

- Always play in the same direction
- Change roles (defender becomes attacker and vice versa)
- Pay attention to the work-rest ratio
- Play with and without offside rule
- Play with and without goalkeeper/line/small goals
- Dimensions 35 x 20 yards, or fresh attackers and a fresh defender 35 yards from goal (to optimize work-rest ratio; see diagram D5.).

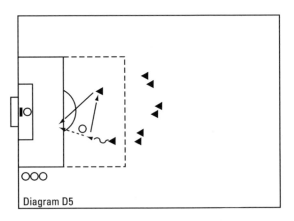

Diagram D5

POSSESSION
Attack

E

3 v 2 (see diagram E1)
Objective:

For the 3 players to score as quickly as possible.

PS * This game is primarily aimed at improving passing
skills when faced with a number of soccer obstacles
and soccer objectives

    * A number of remarks are identical to those given in
the 5 v 2 game (see B.)

What a coach sees:	What the coach does/says:
1. Players pass the ball around without creating any scoring chances (the defenders are able to resist for too long) 2. The ball is passed inaccurately, possession is sometimes lost and the play is not direct enough 3. The defenders are beaten too easily - there is no challenge for them	1. "The purpose of the exercise is to score as quickly as possible." "Play the ball more quickly to each other" Limit the number of times the ball may be touched (e.g. 2-touch or 1-touch play) "Spread out, you are too far apart, the defenders have too much time to take up position". 2. Pay more attention to technical aspects: pace of the ball, direction of play, playing along the ground, passing to teammate's stronger foot, dummy runs (especially off the ball). Take up better positions, don't run behind the defenders, take up new positions all the time". 3. "Close down the space" Limit the attackers by restricting the number of times they can touch the ball, applying the offside rule, introducing a time limit. **Other variations can be added, e.g.** * introduce a goalkeeper (see diagram E2) * force defenders to win the ball as quickly as possible

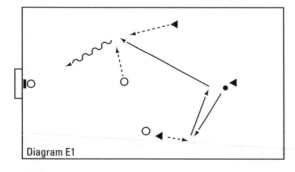

Diagram E1

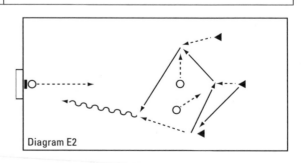

Diagram E2

Organization:

- Continuously alternating defenders (work-rest ratio)
- Alternating groups of 3 (see diagram E3)

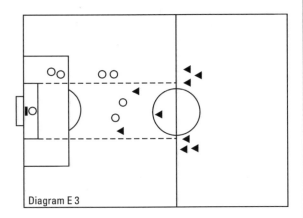

Diagram E 3

- Always play in the same direction
- Defenders can score by intercepting and:
  * dribbling across the line
  * playing a long ball up field to a teammate (see diagram E4)

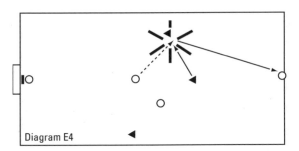

Diagram E4

Especially suitable for beginners:
- Emphasize technical aspects
- Objective is simple (i.e. to score)
- Good coaching of ball control, speed, feel for the ball, direction, taking up position relative to the ball.

This game requires adequate resistance from the defender and places high demands on ball control!

The game can also be played as a competitive game: e.g. the three attackers have to score as quickly as possible, because behind them an additional defender is rushing back to help the other defenders (effectively 3 v 3). The defenders must therefore try to hold up the attackers (see diagram E5).

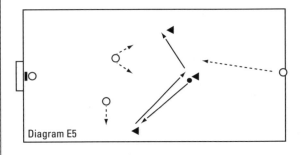

Diagram E5

The striker has often been confronted with this situation during training sessions.

OPPOSITION IN POSSESSION
Defense

1 v 1 (see diagram F1)
Objective:
• To prevent the attacker from scoring and to regain the ball.

F

What a coach sees:	What the coach does/says:
1. The defender is unable to win the ball	1. "Don't approach your opponent too quickly, be cautious - creep up on him" "Get close to your opponent more quickly" "If you wait too long he'll kick the ball past you into the goal, challenge him" "Don't be fooled by his feints, keep alert, keep your knees bent, etc." "Choose the right moment to take/win the ball": * After the defender feints to challenge * When opponent makes an error (e.g. plays the ball too far in front) "Stay eye to eye with your opponent for as long as possible" "Don't turn your back on him" "Stay on your feet as long as possible"
2. The defender is beaten	2. "Try to get back as quickly as possible" "Try to force your opponent wide" "Chase after your opponent and force him to make errors" * Examples of such errors are: poor shot stumbling over the ball "Win the ball by making a sliding tackle"
3. The defender wins the ball	3. "Switch quickly to attack" "Try to score as quickly as possible" "Cut across your opponent's path, keep the ball as far as possible away from him" "Get the ball onto your stronger foot" "Head straight for goal and don't let your self be pushed off the ball"

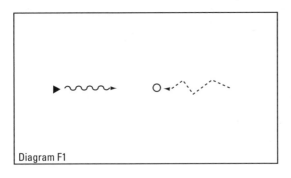
Diagram F1

Organization:
- The organization and approach depend on the objectives, the ability level of the players, and the age of the players.
- The main considerations are:
  - There must be lots of situations where players are beaten or avoid being beaten
  - The game must be rewarding for the players in terms of scoring goals, winning possession, etc.
  - There must be a relationship to "real" match situations
- 1 v 1 game of line soccer in marked-out playing area; 1 v 1 with goals (see diagram C2.); 1 v 1 with full-size goal + goalkeeper (see diagram C3.)
- Change the pairings so that the players do not always face the same opponent.

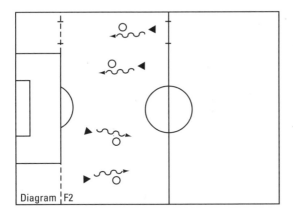
Diagram F2

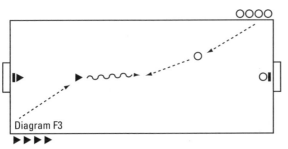
Diagram F3

- Follow up 1 v 1 with:
  - attempt on goal
  - cross
  - pass
- Swap roles after change of possession (a soccer skill)
- The player in possession should initially be given ample opportunity to score or dribble across the line
- The scoring opportunities should then be limited by shortening the line or making the goal smaller
- The work-rest ratio is important in this game. Fatigue has a negative effect on the execution of the move (inability to get past the defender, difficulty in switching from attack to defense, general lack of mobility); try a maximum of 30 - 60 seconds work and then 1 - 2 minutes active rest (e.g. practicing ball skills). The coach should watch out for signs of tiredness (shortage of breath, need to stop, lack of alertness, increased mistakes, etc.).

Even the youngest players learn to challenge for the ball.

OPPOSITION IN POSSESSION
Defense

G

2 v 1 (see diagram G1)

Objectives:

- To prevent the 2 players from scoring (or getting past the defender) and to try to win the ball.
- In any case to screen the goal and gain time (possibly until help arrives).

KEY TO SYMBOLS	
▼	Team in possession
O	Team not in possession
——►	Pass (path of the ball)
∿∿►	Player dribbles
- - -►	Player makes a run

What a coach sees:	What the coach does/says:
1. The defender is beaten too easily	1. "Don't challenge the player in possession too quickly (don't dive in)" "Try to delay both players, keep them both in view, win time"
2. The defender cannot prevent the player in possession from scoring	2. "Always choose to defend the most dangerous situations, and always try to get between the ball and the goal"
3. The attackers have too many options for getting past the defender (skillful attackers)	3. "Try to use your initiative; pressure the attackers by feinting to challenge; keep them busy" Applying the offside rule will make it easier for the defender but more difficult for the attackers Make the playing area narrower
4. The defender always ends up on the ground when he challenges for the ball	4. "Stay on your feet, stay mobile; if you go down you're beaten"
5. When the defender wins the ball he almost immediately loses it again	5. "Try to screen the ball, try to get to the touchline or the goal line" (to provoke a throw-in or corner kick) "Try to reach your teammate(s) further up field by playing an accurate long ball" (see scoring exercise G2) "Try to score by breaking out, keep your opponents away from the ball"

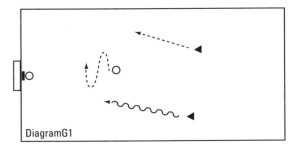

DiagramG1

Diagram G2.: If the defender wins the ball he can score by passing the ball directly to a striker.

Organization:
- Always play in the same direction
- Pay attention to the work-rest ratio
- Use lines as goal, or small goals or full-size goals with goalkeeper
- Use extra player to pass the ball to, when it has been won (long ball, see diagram G2.)

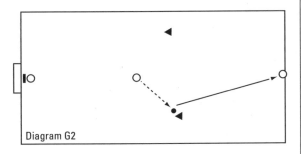

Diagram G2

- Use an extra defender who runs back to assist, creating a 2 v 2 situation (see diagram G3)

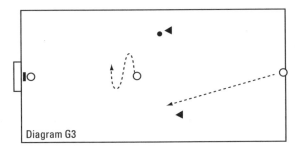

Diagram G3

- Allow the players to play in all the different roles

Asking for the ball
(4 shots in sequence)

Face the teammate who has the ball.

Confuse the marker by moving out of his line of view.

Ask for the ball at the right moment (communication with teammate).

Screen the ball from the marker when you receive it.

OPPOSITION IN POSSESSION
Defense

H

3 v 2 (see diagram H1)
Objectives:

- To prevent the 3 players from scoring (or from getting past the defenders) and to try to win the ball.
- To emphasize the concept of regaining the ball (so-called "active" defending - the ball has to be regained).
  PS See also the comments for the 2 v 1 and 3 v 2 games!

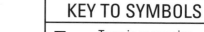

What a coach sees:	What the coach does/says:
1. The defenders are beaten too quickly	1. "Don't go in too quickly, don't go for the ball too soon" Choose the right moment to win the ball: * inaccurate pass by opponent * opponent plays the ball too hard to his teammate "Cover each other's backs, work together" "Communicate with each other"
2. The attackers repeatedly beat the defenders by going down the flanks	2. "Don't play too close to each other"
3. The attackers repeatedly beat the defenders by going through the middle	3. "Play closer to each other and cover each other's backs"
4. The defenders cannot retain possession once the ball has been won	4. "Once you have worked the ball into space, try to hit a good long ball" "Play the ball quickly to a teammate who is in a better position (usually further back and therefore with more space) to play a long ball (to an extra teammate up front)"
5. The defenders are too easily beaten	5. The attackers have to deal with the offside rule and perhaps a narrower field of play

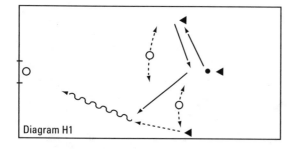

Diagram H1

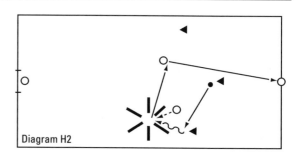

Diagram H2

Diagram H2.:
Winning the ball and playing a long pass.

Organization:

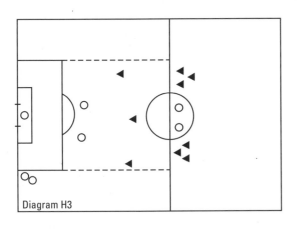

Diagram H3

- Always play in the same direction
- Pay attention to the work-rest ratio
- Use lines as goals, or smaller goals or full-size goal with a goalkeeper
- Use an extra player to pass the ball to, when it has been won (long ball, see diagram H2.)
- Continuously introduce new sets of three players (see diagram H3.)
- Competitive game by asking attackers to score as quickly as possible (e.g. last minute of match)
- Competitive game by asking the defenders to win the ball as quickly as possible (last minute of the match, and their team is losing)

Intercept the ball, and hold onto it!

OPPOSITION IN POSSESSION
Defense

4 v 3 (see diagram I1)

Objectives:

- To prevent the 4 players from scoring (or from getting past the defenders) and to try to win the ball.
- To emphasize the concept of regaining the ball (so-called "active" defending - the ball has to be regained).

  P.S. See also the comments for the 2 v 1 and 3 v 2 games!

KEY TO SYMBOLS	
▼	Team in possession
O	Team not in possession
→	Pass (path of the ball)
∿►	Player dribbles
‑ ‑ ‑►	Player makes a run

What a coach sees:	What the coach does/says:
1. The defenders wait too long and only win the ball when the attackers make mistakes	1. "You have to win the ball even though you have one man less" "Stay close to each other, especially near the ball" "Cut off the passing options close to the ball" "Don't mark the fourth attacker, who is further away from the ball, but watch him closely"
2. The defenders always choose the wrong moment to challenge for the ball and are always beaten	2. "Pick the right moment to challenge for the ball; try to create the chance your self by feinting to challenge" "Keep reading the situation, and take action when a bad pass is made (too hard, too gentle, too inaccurate) by chasing after the ball"
3. The defenders have too little chance of winning the ball (attackers are too skillful)	3. A completely different situation can be created by introducing the offside rule or narrowing the size
4. The defenders lose the ball too quickly after they have won it	4. When a defender has possession the two other defenders must take up positions (usually by moving backwards) which will allow them to play a long ball (to an extra teammate, see diagram I2.)
5. The defenders are forced back too close to their own goal	5. A longer field of play and instructions to win the ball as quickly as possible makes things more difficult for the defenders
6. The defender who most frequently plays the ball back lets himself be pushed back and therefore gives the attackers too much space	6. Teach the last defender how to use the off side rule, stop, warn, anticipate, etc.

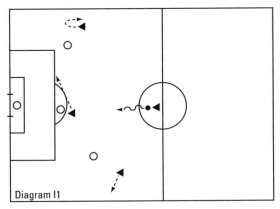

Diagram I1

Diagram I3.: 6 v 8, after winning the ball the defenders can score by playing a direct long ball to a player over the halfway line. (Adapt size of pitch to suit quality of players)

Organization:

- A number of teams of 4, with each player occupying the position corresponding to his position in the full (11-man) team, play in turns on a pitch which is the width of the penalty area and half the length of a full pitch (see diagram I2)

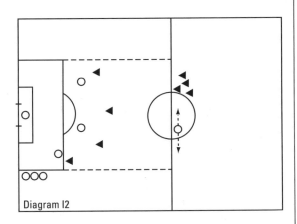

Diagram I2

- The three defenders try to win the ball back as soon as possible, and can score by playing a long pass to an extra player positioned over the halfway line (ball can be played along the ground or in the air)
- Offside rule can be applied to aid defenders.

- This game can be made more complex by playing 8 attackers against 6 defenders (see diagram I3). In this case the offside rule should be applied and the full width of the pitch should be used. Another method of scoring can be introduced (e.g. defenders dribble the ball across the halfway line)
- In the 8 v 6 game the main consideration is how the organization, the formation and the positions of the players are realized.

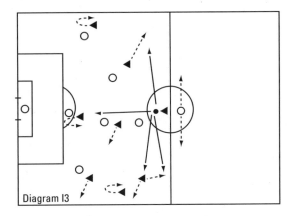

Diagram I3

Winning the ball back as quickly as possible is also

FAIR PLAY

K N V B

POSSESSION AND OPPOSITION POSSESSION
Buildup, attacking and defensive
4 v 4 (see diagram J1)

J

Objective: To confront the players with, and coach them in how to deal with, the obstacles/difficulty factors which they will encounter in real matches; the emphasis can be varied per training session depending on what you want to achieve with the group (level, age, position in league competition, etc.); the players must realize that soccer problems are first and foremost their own concern.

KEY TO SYMBOLS

▼	Team in possession
○	Team not in possession
→	Pass (path of the ball)
∿►	Player dribbles
- - -►	Player makes a run

Ia. OWN TEAM IN POSSESSION (team as a whole)

What a coach sees:	What the coach does/says:
	(Choice of words should be different for 6-year-olds than 17-year-olds)
1. No scoring chances are created	1. "The game's about winning!" "If you want to win you have to score goals"
2. The ball is persistently played square or back	2. "You have to get close to the opposition's goal"
3. The players don't stay in position	3. Players must stay in their own position: "Stay in position!"
4. There is not enough communication with each other	4. "Let's hear your voice" Use terms such as: "Take your time" - there's no opponent close to you "Man on" - an opponent is closing in "Pass" - I'm open, you can give me the ball
5. The opposing players are not pulled out of position	5. "Go on your own" - beat your man - this can open up a goal chance or create a numerical advantage "Move the ball around faster in the buildup" "Create as much space as possible" "Use all the space available"
6. The game becomes totally aimless	6. "Don't all go for the ball - that just draws opponents towards the ball, making the situation too tight and therefore more difficult"

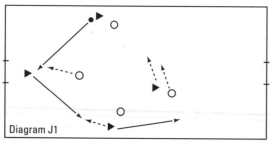

Diagram J1

Ib OWN TEAM IN POSSESSION (player who has the ball)

What a coach sees:	What the coach does/says:
1. Player in possession fails to confront opponent	1. "Take your opponent on, try to beat him"
2. Player in possession doesn't try to feint	2. "Threaten to take the ball in a certain direction, try to use a feint to get past your opponent"
3. Player with the ball feints too soon	3. "Don't feint too soon" "Try to be more relaxed as you approach your opponent"
4. Player with the ball feints too late	4. "Feint at the right moment, otherwise the ball will be blocked"
5. Inaccurate passing - teammates have difficulty controlling the ball and this slows down the play	5. "Pass the ball more accurately" "You are hitting the ball too hard/too gently" "Play the ball to your teammate's stronger foot" "Don't play the ball to the side where the marker is standing" "Play the ball along the ground" "Lay the ball off first time" "Keep it simple, use the inside of your foot" "Try to weight the pass properly" "Look around before you receive the ball, try to anticipate" "Communicate with each other, tell them where you want the ball" The coach decides to increase the size of the playing area
6. Player in possession is not calm enough	6. "Take your time, there's nobody on you"
7. Player in possession does not know what to do next	7. "Goalkeeper, teammates, tell him what to do"

The main job of the center forward is to score.

Ic. OWN TEAM IN POSSESSION (players who do not have the ball)

What a coach sees:	What the coach does/says:
1. Player in possession has no passing options	1. Comments to players in the immediate vicinity of the player in possession: "Run into space, make yourself available" "Look as if you want the ball, ask for the ball" "Force him to pass to you" "Choose the right moment to run into space/make yourself available" "Run confidently into space/sprint free of your marker" "Make space for yourself - first move away from the ball and then double back towards it, and vice versa" "Try to run into space without your opponent noticing" "Be prepared for the next move, stay involved, you're still needed"
2. Player in possession can only play the ball square or back	2. "Take up a position which enables a long ball to be played - move away from the ball, then double back towards it"
3. Player in possession can only kick the ball up field	3. "Try to keep the ball, use the space towards your own goal" "Sweeper/full-back - take up position further behind the ball" "Goalkeeper, make sure that the ball can be played back to you, stay involved"
4. In restart situations the disorganization of the opposition is not exploited quickly enough	4. "Put your hand on the ball and look around and/or play the ball quickly" "Grab the ball quickly, hand the ball over, run into space quickly, take the ball quickly"

We have the ball now. Don't go towards the ball, run into space number 11!

II OPPOSITION IN POSSESSION

What a coach sees:	What the coach does/says:
1. Players give the opposition too many scoring chances	1. "Don't let him shoot" "Get into the path of the shot" "The man on the ball is the most dangerous" "Tackle him" "Block the shot" In heading duels: "Try to head the ball away" "Jump with him", "Go for it" "Don't duck your head" "Keep your eyes on the ball", "Use your body"
2. Marking is poor	2. "Stay on your man" "Don't let him get behind your back" "Get back" "Don't give your opponent a chance to pass or receive a pass" "Get behind the ball, make yourself useful for the team" "Mark more closely, get on the right side of your man" "Mark more closely near the ball, try to prevent the pass"
3. There are too few players near the ball to mark closely: they are beaten	3. "Don't dive in, try to gain time, delay your opponent, stay calm" "Stay on your feet, keep your knees bent" "We need an extra defender to give cover" "Mark the most important opponents" "Cover his back" "Force him out wide"
4. Markers don't put enough effort into winning the ball back	4. "Make it harder for him" "Defend actively" "Feint to make a challenge" "Close them down" - force them towards the by-line or into a corner. "Communicate with each other" e.g. "Stay in front, hold it, etc."
5. Free-kicks are conceded while defending	5. "Play the ball, not the man" "Only make a sliding tackle if you are sure you'll win the ball" "Keep your hands to yourself"
6. The opposition takes advantage of the disorganization at restart situations	6. "Keep your eyes on the ball" "Watch your opponent closely"

III TRANSITION FROM OWN TEAM IN POSSESSION TO OPPOSITION IN POSSESSION (ball is lost)

What a coach sees:	What the coach does/says:
1. Players don't switch quickly enough from attack to defense 2. Possession is lost (general) 3. The ball is lost after a goal scoring attempt/close to opposition's goal	1. "Get back quickly, make yourself useful for the team" 2. "Get behind the ball" 3. Depends on the match situation/objective of the exercise: e.g. if you are losing then you have to regain the ball: "Stay where you are, mark closely" "Keep things tight, keep up the pressure" "Close down all passing options, close down the space" "Link up from the back, push up" "Goalkeeper, move further out of your goal, you are the sweeper now" Another example: You want to hold on to your lead: "Fall back into your own half, regroup, wait for the opposition to make an error" "Close down the space at the back"
4. The ball is lost on or around the halfway line	4. "Get back as quickly as possible" "The player closest to the ball offers the first resistance" "Close them down, get closer together"
5. The ball is lost close to the team's own goal during the initial buildup	5. "Come out towards the ball as quickly as possible" "The player closest to the ball must try to offer the first resistance" "Close them down, get closer together" "Don't mark the players on the flanks" "Screen your own goal" "Force them to play square and/or back" "Force them out to the flanks"

Pressure your opponent as soon as the ball is lost.

IIIb CHANGE OF POSSESSION (winning the ball)

What a coach sees:	What the coach does/says:
1. Possession is won (general)	1. Remarks to players depend on the circumstances: * Can opponents put pressure on the man in possession? * Does the ball have to be got under control first? * Do the other players have to create space first? * Can the ball be played up field? * Does the ball have to be played square or back?
2. The ball is won, but there are lots of opponents nearby	2. "Communicate with each other" (e.g. screen the ball) "Run into space with the ball" "Watch out for the player behind you" "Pass back/square" "Clear the ball/kick it up field" "Take up a good position/run into space so that the ball can be played to you" "Call for the ball"
3. The ball is won close to the opposition's goal	3. Depends once again on the circumstances, e.g. current scoreline, position of opponent: "Try to shoot at goal, score" "Try to hold the ball there" "Try to get to the goal line" "Try to pass to a teammate who is in a scoring position" "Try to win a corner"
4. The ball is won close to the team's own goal	4. "Try to reach a striker with a first-time pass" "Sprint forward with the ball so that you can't be tackled" "Calm the situation down, allow teammates to get into position (including the goalkeeper)"

VARIATIONS ON 4 V 4 ARE DESCRIBED IN DETAIL IN CHAPTER 8

EXAMPLES OF TRAINING SESSIONS FOR JUNIORS BASED ON SOCCER PROBLEMS

KEY TO SYMBOLS

▼	Team in possession
○	Team not in possession
→	Pass (path of the ball)
∿▶	Player dribbles
- - -▶	Player makes a run

EXAMPLE 1

Main problem

1. Keeping possession when faced with the following obstacles: space (small/large), opponents (few/many), direction of play, objectives (buildup/scoring/maintaining the lead).

2. Keeping possession to facilitate optimal buildup through good positional play so that scoring chances can be created.

Practice plan

5 v 2 / 6 v 3 / 5 v 3

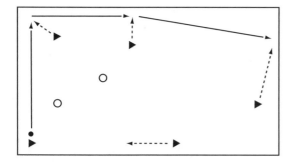

- The 5 (or 6) players try to keep possession by passing and taking up positions.
- The 2 (or 3) opponents try to win the ball.

Coaching: concentrate on technical execution of passing, and receiving passes.

5 v 2 / 5 v 3

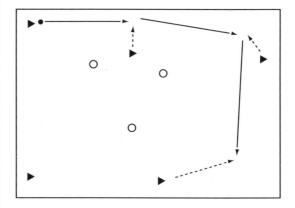

- The 5 players must pass the ball 10 times to each other without the ball being touched by the defenders or letting the ball go outside the rectangle.
- The 2 or 3 defenders can score by winning the ball and dribbling it out of the rectangle.

Coaching:
concentrate on the direction of play: "Play the ball where there are no defenders".

The match provides the real test.

3 v 2

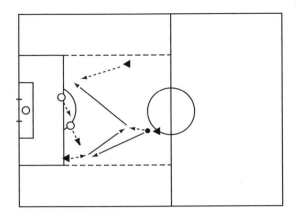

- The 3 players must score from chances they have created with passing moves, etc.
- The 2 defenders can score by dribbling the ball across the line! They can only lose the ball when a goal is scored!

Coaching:
- Speed of goal scoring attempts
- Increase obstacles by making the playing area smaller and applying the offside rule.

This game is all about scoring goals!

3 v 1 / 3 v 2 + 1 v 1 in front of goal

- The 3 players must cooperate to create space to play the long ball under pressure from the opponent; one player must be played free.
- The striker has to choose the right moment to ask for the ball. Follow buildup closely.

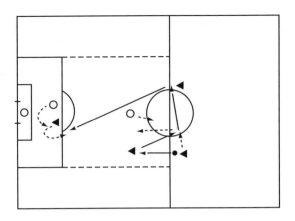

EXAMPLE 2

Main problem

The players must learn how to work together as a team to win the ball back when the opposition has possession. Important aspects in different zones of the playing area are position, tasks and responsibilities.

Practice plan

8 v 7 / 8 v 6

- Make it clear to the players that they must work together when their opponents have possession.
- The 8 cannot play 1 against 1 but must try to win the ball back by good communication and good positional play -> play close to each other -> close down opponents' space

Coaching:
- Get behind the ball
- Close down space
- Communicate with each other
- Choose the right moment to win the ball
- Stay close to the ball -> apply pressure/chase the ball
- Do not concede free-kicks

EXAMPLE 3

Main problem

1. Attackers must score more goals from in and around the penalty area.
2. Defenders must defend their own goal and win the ball back.

The coach has to devise a practice situation in which the players can learn to solve the problems. The problem as described above demands the following practice situation:

- Invitation to score goals/prevent goals being scored:
  - Easy scoring opportunities
  - More resistance from extra defenders/less space.
- Special technical/tactical skills:
  - Dribbling -> holding the ball; screening the ball; stronger foot; etc.
  - Shooting -> good position; initial stride.
  - Goal-orientedness -> take the most direct route to goal.
  - Defending -> choose the right moment, no fouls; good tackling technique.

After beating an opponent... there is still another obstacle.

1 v 1

A starts with a dribble and scores.

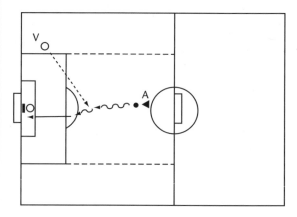

V sets off a little later and tries to stop A; if he wins the ball he can score in a small goal.

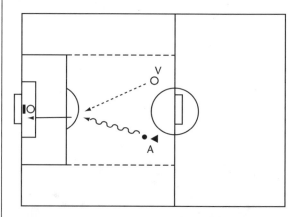

A starts with a dribble and scores
V comes from another position and tries to stop A, etc. Now there is more pressure on the ball.

Coaching: Increase resistance by manipulating the space.

2 v 2

A1 and A2 score by:

- Dribbling.
- Taking the ball over.
- Playing a wall-pass.

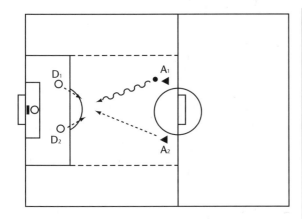

- Individual run; after creating space
- V1 and V2 try to prevent a goal being scored:
  - use good tackling technique
  - then go on to score

Coaching: Draw players' attention to detail; technical aspects -> dribbling and shooting.

EXAMPLE 4

Main problem
1. Defenders must improve their defending:
- Prevent goals/cover the route to goal.
- Win ball - defend actively - try to influence the attackers by feinting to tackle.
  The defenders show a lack of knowledge of their task/function.
  Their defensive technique is not good enough to win the ball.
2. Cooperation between defenders and attackers must improve (communication) because:
  - the defenders' passes don't reach the attackers;
  - poor timing when asking for the ball/passing the ball; poor exploitation of the situation; inability to mislead opponents.

The coach must devise a practice situation in which the defenders are forced to defend better, i.e. more pressure needs to be exerted on defenders.
E.g. your team is losing, but needs to win to become champion or avoid being knocked out of the cup competition.

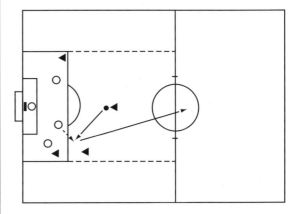

- Defenders must win the ball.
- Defenders can score by kicking the ball through the air into the zone or the small goal (this is the purpose of winning the ball).

Coaching:
Timing of challenge for the ball.
- Work together to create space for playing the long ball.

The coach must devise a practice situation which requires good cooperation between defenders and attackers

3 v 1 + striker/defender

- Pressure on defenders; opponents try to disrupt buildup play.
- Attackers must choose the right moment to ask for the ball (-> move, call), remain in control of the buildup (-> concentration).
- If this goes well, increase resistance from opponents.

KEY TO SYMBOLS

▼ Team in possession
○ Team not in possession
→ Pass (path of the ball)
⌇⌇⌇► Player dribbles
- - -► Player makes a run

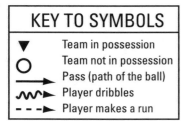

3 v 1 -> 1 v 1 -> 4 v 2 in front of

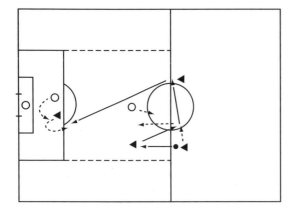

Subsequently expand to:

3 v 2/3 v 3 + 2 strikers/2 defenders

Also carry out towards the touch lines:

- Right back -> right winger
- Left back -> left winger

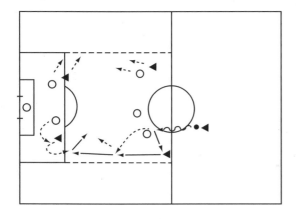

EXAMPLE 5

Main problem

1. The players must learn how to work together as a team when in possession -> in order to win the match (i.e. score goals).
2. As 1, but when opposition has possession (for description see above)
   - In front of team's own goal.
   - In midfield.
   - In front of opposition's goal.

The coach picks out soccer problems from the game.

The coach must devise a practice situation in which it is essential to perform better as a team.

Coaching plan
Small sided games with goalkeepers

- Simplified games derived from "real" soccer games -> 7 v 7 / 8 v 8
- Accentuate the importance of team work by playing uneven sides e.g. 8 v 7 / 8 v 6.

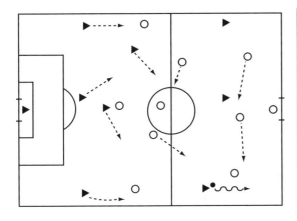

COACHING

Own team in possession (attacking)
- Spread out.
- Create space in all directions.
- Stay in position.
- Read the game -> choose the right moment to ask for the ball.
- Go through on your own because there is no one to stop you.
- Keep passing at a high tempo to drag opponents out of position.

Opposition in possession
- Get behind the ball.
- Close down space -> stay close to each other.

Block the pass.

- Communicate with each other.
- Read the game -> pick out the right moment to win the ball.
- Close to the ball -> pressure opponents/chase the ball
- Away from the ball -> keep in contact with each other and opponents.
- Try to disrupt opponents' play.
- Don't concede free-kicks; you will never gain possession that way.
- Defend well technically.

EXAMPLE 6

Main problems

1. Pre-season preparation (approx. 4 to 5 week time period); a general problem.
a. Improving general physical condition
b. Specific coaching aimed at defending in midfield (corresponding with the development of the playing concept), and which also improves general physical condition.

Description

Stage 1.

A general warming-up session which includes limbering-up in combination with stretching exercises and general preliminary strength-building exercises.

Prerequisites of a soccer training session:

1. Typical soccer objectives.

2. Constant repetition.

3. Take group aspects into consideration.

4. Correct coaching.

Stage 2.

Defense v attackers including:

a. An instructive session (understanding the objective, analyzing the situation).
b. A practical session in which various coaching methods are used (modifying the size of the playing area, rules and other obstacles).

Practice plan defending - attacking

Slightly smaller playing area

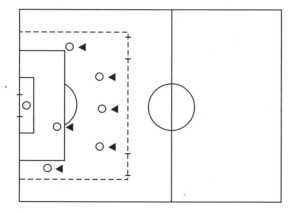

Game plan:

- Defenders build up a move with the aim of scoring by dribbling the ball across the opponents' goal line or taking it through two small goals on the goal line.
- Attackers defend zonally, switching to man-to-man marking: challenge for the ball, harass and chase the man in possession; score when in possession. Buildup play always starts with the goalkeeper (throw or goal kick).

EXAMPLE 7

Main problem

The team plays with a tight defense: one striker and everyone else behind the ball. This means that players have to make forward runs from the midfield and defensive lines (1-2 combination, individual run, crossfield pass).
Ability to score while under pressure from chasing opponent is poor:

- Nervousness, inability to make decisions.
- Defender is given another chance (by not cutting across him).
- Not fit enough; lack of pace and stamina.

Description

General warming-up in preparation for training session, concentrating on speed and stamina (quite rigorous, placing heavy demands on certain muscles).
Again by means of general running/ coordination and strength-building exercises.

This is only possible after a thorough warm-up.

Stage 2.

An isolated game, in which the problem is practiced. Learn to read the situation.

Sequence:

The attacker begins with a few yards start on the following defender. He can either take the ball on himself or play a 1-2 combination.

He finds himself in 1 v 1 situation with the goalkeeper; the defender stays with him all the way to the goal line and tries to get behind the goalkeeper.

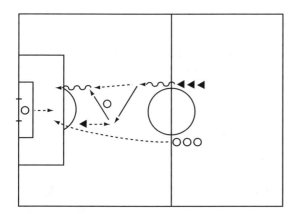

Situation 2

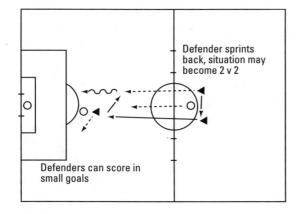

Defender sprints back, situation may become 2 v 2

Defenders can score in small goals

Other examples of soccer problems

1. Players return from their summer vacation, and start their first week of preparation for the new season.

Within a few weeks the team must be capable of playing matches at a competitive level. There are 3 weeks of preparation, during which training sessions are held 3 times each week and there are 3 practice matches.

2. The strikers are easily pushed off the ball when they sprint into space to receive a long ball from the defenders or mid-fielders -> i.e. possession is lost.

3. The winger often beats his opponent but then only rarely delivers a good cross or threatens the goal. His opponent is often able to recover.

4. The team is not very good at winning the ball back in the opposition's half. Some players always arrive just too late to prevent the player in possession from getting out of trouble by good positional play, by hitting a long forward pass, or by passing back to the goalkeeper or a defender.

5. The goalkeeper does not switch quickly enough once he has won the ball by catching a cross, saving a shot on goal or intercepting a through ball. He cannot throw or kick the ball out a accurately, so the opposition has time to regroup.

6. When the team wins the ball and starts its buildup play in defense, the defenders need so much time on the ball that they have few opportunities to play a long pass, despite the fact that their strikers take up good positions.

7. The defenders and midfield players always arrive too late to support the strikers when they have received a long ball. If the forwards hold onto the ball, too much time is wasted before the attack can be continued.

If the strikers lose the ball, the gap between them and the midfield and defense is too large, allowing the opposition the freedom to build up from the back.

8. A midfielder consistently tries to win the ball from an opponent with a sliding tackle, usually without success. He then finds himself on the ground and cannot recover quickly enough.

9. When the opposition has possession, the team usually has difficulty in exerting pressure, so the ball can never be won back effectively. The opposition is given the freedom to build up, so the ball is only regained in and around the team's penalty area, when an opponent makes an error.

10. When the team has possession in its defensive zone, there are frequently no options for playing the ball up field. The strikers and midfielders fail to take up good positions. They take no initiatives in moving towards the opposition's goal.

11. The defenders must improve their defending. They are too easily beaten in 1 v 1 situations. They concede too many free-kicks and hardly ever win the ball.

12. The defenders pay too much attention to their "own" attacker. They do not have the insight to take the most useful option, e.g. leaving their man when he moves out towards the flank, and providing cover.

Soccer can be learned better against real opponents.

CHAPTER 7
TECHNIQUE IN SOCCER

Technique is always linked to the objectives of the game. It is, by definition, goal-oriented. It is a means to an end.

The objectives of the game must first be understood before we can say anything about technique.

Soccer technique is the means of controlling the ball, and it cannot be described, discussed or taught except in this context. A comparison can be drawn with, for example, driving a car. The only way to learn to drive a car is by practicing it in traffic.

Everything the student driver is taught is aimed at enabling him to get from point A to point B. The instructor does not ask him to take the steering wheel home to practice with, because that has nothing to do with the problem.

Technique is learning to control the ball.

The same applies to learning how to play soccer. As soon as youngsters are capable of controlling the ball to some degree, they should practice their technical skills in real soccer situations. Only in this way can players learn to use technique as a means to an end. Technique is a tool which enables the game to be played. It can be used to carry out simple tasks (young beginners) and to solve very complex soccer problems (top players).

Practice (doing it) is the best teacher, but it must be organized in such a way that players can learn as much as possible. By adapting the dimensions of the pitch, the rules of the game, and the size of the goals, a coach can focus on specific technical skills (see the variations of 4 v 4 in chapter 8).

Players learn to apply technical skills flexibly if they regularly play types of games in which they are repeatedly required to apply specific technical skills. No two situations are the same in a game of soccer, and this is why players have to develop their technique by actually playing. There is no 'ideal' technique: how a player kicks the ball with his instep will always depend on the options available to him, his position on the field, and the positions of his teammates and opponents.

Skilled coaching is necessary to achieve the best returns in the limited period available (1 or 2 hours per week). Skilled coaching costs time and must be approached systematically and methodically.

The coach must:

- Have a thorough knowledge of the basic techniques.

- Have the ability to simplify soccer situations or make them more difficult.

- Have good coaching skills.

- Keep up to date with the demands made on soccer coaching.

What happens, however, if:

- A practice drill is not popular, its objective is not understood (what is the point of this exercise?), or the players do not enjoy it, so that the learning process is hindered and the drill loses its point?

- The object of a basic game cannot be achieved ("the game is not played") because the players do not have enough technical skill or insight, or do not know how to communicate with each other, and therefore do not learn anything (the game is too difficult)?

The coach puts himself literally on the same level as the players.

Obviously measures then have to be taken so that the game can be played properly.

- Explain the objective of the game (in the context of the situations "own team in possession" and

"opponents in possession"; see Chapter 5).

- Make the game simpler by removing or adapting obstacles:
  - organization/dimensions of pitch;
  - number of players;
  - number of opponents.

- Give instructions/corrections/examples.

Practice makes perfect

Basic techniques

In the case of the youngest players, it is clear that the major "problem" is learning to control the ball. We say that the ball is a "first-order obstacle". When these players (aged 6 to 9 years) start to play soccer, they have to learn how to master the ball.

They have to learn how a ball rolls, how hard or soft it is, etc. In this phase players have to learn how they can pass, kick, dribble, push, receive, stop, head and shoot the ball, and how to combine all these skills. It is impossible to devote too much time to practicing with the ball with players of this age. Above all, the players should practice on their own initiative: at home, in the street, in the playground, in the park, etc.

Methodical sequence for learning soccer skills

5 - 7 years old (aim: learning to control the ball)

1. Movement exercises/games designed to promote familiarity with the ball.

2. Basic games which ensure lots of ball

contacts:
- small numbers of players (1 v 1, 2 v 1, 2 v 2, with/without goalkeeper, line soccer);
- simple soccer situations (aiming at a target, moving quickly with the ball, etc.).

3. Coaching in the technical execution of these simple situations.

7 - 12 years old
(aim: basic proficiency)

1. Basic games
   4 v 4 + variations -> objectives + clear explanation of the organization of these games + keeping the game flowing (as prerequisite for learning/developing).

2. Coaching in these situations, with the accent on coaching in technique.

12 - 16 years old
(aim: competitive proficiency)

1. Match situations:
   - Real matches.
   - Practice situations: 8 v 8.
   - "Freeze" situations: stopping the play and taking it forward in slow motion (question and answer).

2. Task training
   a. General: 3 main moments.
   b. Specific: by position, line, flank.

3. Basic games focusing more on specific aspects of each task/function (technical development proceeds, but more specifically targeted at the player's possibilities for his position during the match).

4. Mental training:
   - Team-building/being able to play within the limitations of a given task.

- Making individual qualities subordinate to the interests of the team as a whole.
- Making an investment (practicing) with a view to gaining the rewards later.

General methods available to the coach:

- Organizing and initiating basic games.
- Recognizing, naming and coaching/ teaching technical components of the game.
- Manipulating obstacles (making them easier or harder).
- Applying theoretical knowledge.
- Using video tapes.
- Setting an example (either himself or through a good player).

The coach must not try to persuade his charges that there is a simpler way to play. Imparting any form of technical skill requires considerable insight into the game. Learning to play soccer is a "doing" activity, which is only restricted by the time available. It cannot be made any simpler than it is.

And ... the shorter the available time, the greater the need for coaching.

Soccer Technique

Technique is a means
Technique, insight and communication (TIC) cannot be separated
➥ Aim to illustrate objectives within context of the 3 main moments in a soccer match.

Tasks/Functions	Observable behavior	M E A N S				Emphasized in	
		Required Technical Skills	General description of technique	Insight	Commun-ication	Practice and competitive games	Small Sided Game
Possession							
<u>Defenders & Goalkeeper</u> • Initiate buildup	<u>Positional play</u> • Everyone in position (keep team shape) • Switching the play • Aim to play as far upfield as possible • Controlled ball circulation • Pushing out towards the edges of the playing area • No loss of possession ➥ No risks	• passing/kicking (short/long) • receiving and controlling the ball	See Chapter 8 + Goalkeeper Chapter 9	See Chpts. 1/5/11 + keeper Chpt. 9	See Chpts. 1/5/11 + keeper Chpt. 9	Positional game • 5 v 2 • 4 v 3 / 5 v 4 to goal ➥ defending 2 goals / playing to striker, etc. • Positional game ➥ Playing to strikers ➥ Linking up	• 4 v 4 basic game • 4 small goals (2 yards from corner flag) • long/narrow field • 6 v 6 / 8 v 8 • 1 full-size goal + 2 small goals
<u>Midfielders</u> • From buildup to attack	• everyone in position in own zone (keep zonal shape) • Get forward when possible • No unnecessary loss of possession ➥ Limited risks • Find space • Shoot if possible (from distance) • Play in penalty area	• receiving the ball / first touch into space (especially for attacking mid-fielder) • passing • dribbling • shooting • heading (attacking)	See Chapter 8 + Goalkeeper Chapter 9	See Chpts. 1/5/11 + keeper Chpt. 9	See Chpts. 1/5/11 + keeper Chpt. 9	• 5 v 2 / 5 v 3 • 4 v 3 / 5 v 4 to goal • Positional game 3 v 2 / 4 v 3 ➥ Playing to strikers ➥ Linking up	• 4 v 4 • 4 small goals • line soccer (whole line) • 4 v 4 with accent on heading/shooting ➥ full-size goals., close to each other • 6 v 6 / 8 v 8 1 full-size goal (+2 small goals / line / play to striker)
<u>Strikers</u> • Attack	• Everyone in position (keep team shape) • Spread out • Leave gaps from teammates (avoid crowding) • Hold the ball • Beat opponent/run off the ball • Finishing • Taking risks	• passing • laying the ball off • receiving the ball / playing it into space • dribbling • beating a man / feinting with the ball Finishing: • shooting • heading/ lobbing/chipping • diving header	See Chapter 8 + Goalkeeper Chapter 9	See Chpts. 1/5/11 + keeper Chpt. 9	See Chpts. 1/5/11 + keeper Chpt. 9	• 4 v 3 / 5 v 4 to goal • positional game 3 v 2 / 4 v 3 ➥ playing to strikers ➥ Linking up	
<u>Wingers</u> • Attack	• Be available • Individual run • Cross • 1-2 combinations	• receiving/con-trolling the ball/feinting with the ball • passing	See Chapter 8 + Goalkeeper Chapter 9	See Chpts. 1/5/11 + keeper Chpt. 9	See Chpts. 1/5/11 + keeper Chpt. 9	• Positional game on wing / in center • Attack and go for goal; defensive line / playing to striker • Both teams try to score in full-size goal	• 4 v 4 • 1 full-size goal (+ 2 small goals / line / play to striker) • 6 v 6 / 8 v 8 attack < - > defense

Soccer Technique

Technique is a means
Technique, insight and communication (TIC) cannot be separated
➟ Aim to illustrate objectives within context of the 3 main moments in a soccer match.

Tasks/Functions	Observable behavior	M E A N S Required Technical Skills	General description of technique	Insight	Commun-ication	Emphasized in Practice and competitive games	Small Sided Game
Opponents in Possession Strikers • Disrupt opponents' buildup	Team Shape • Reduce playing area (close down space) • Prevent forward pass (force square pass) • Pressure defenders • Close down / cover teammates' backs	-> Movement technique in relation to soccer situation • Block forward pass / sliding tackle • Defensive technique -> Do not get beaten; challenge for the ball • Delay / exert pressure (remain useful for as long as possible)	See Chapter 8 + Goalkeeper Chapter 9	See Chpts. 1/5/11 + keeper Chpt. 9	See Chpts. 1/5/11 + keeper Chpt. 9	• Basic game 5 v 2 / 5 v 3 • 3 v 2 positional game + striker (s) to play the ball to • Defense / attack in situations of numerical superiority; 1 full-size goal and line (defenders defend line, strikers defend goal)	• 4 v 4 • Short field -> line soccer (whole line) • Defense against attack • Defenders score on full-size goal + attackers score by dribbling over line
Midfielders • Disrupt opponents' buildup/attack • Regain possession	• Mark tightly • Avoid being beaten • Play close together (organization) • Cover teammates' backs (close down) • Prevent long forward pass • Good defensive positional play	• Defensive technique -> Win the ball / exert pressure -> Blocking Intercept / place body between ball and opponent • Blocking / prevent long forward pass	See Chapter 8 + Goalkeeper Chapter 9	See Chpts. 1/5/11 + keeper Chpt. 9	See Chpts. 1/5/11 + keeper Chpt. 9	• 5 v 2 / 5 v 3 • 3 v 2 / 4 v 3 positional game + striker (s) to play the ball to • down the middle • over the flank	• 3 v 3 / 4 v 4 + Neutral player • 6 v 6 / 8 v 8 • Line soccer (whole line)
Defenders • Prevent scoring attempts • Prevent goals • Regain possession	• Prevent goals • Win the ball (fairly!) • Close down / cover teammates' backs • Mark direct opponent	• Defensive technique -> Win the ball / exert pressure -> Blocking -> Sliding tackle -> Heading (defensive)	See Chapter 8 + Goalkeeper Chapter 9	See Chpts. 1/5/11 + keeper Chpt. 9	See Chpts. 1/5/11 + keeper Chpt. 9	• 1 v 1 • 2 v 1 towards full-size goal • 4 v 3 towards full-size goal + striker (s) to play the ball to • 8 v 7 / 8 v 6 / 7 v 5 / 6 v 4 attack against defense - full size goal + line • 3 v 2 / 4 v 3 + striker(s) to play the ball to • Positional game over flank + strikers / defenders in front of goal	• 4 v 4 • 2 full-size goals (shooting + heading) • 8 v 8 • Full-size goal • line / playing to striker
Goalkeeper • Prevent goals • Regain possession	• Defend goal • Gain possession		See Chapter 8 + Goalkeeper Chapter 9	See Chpts. 1/5/11 + keeper Chpt. 9	See Chpts. 1/5/11 + keeper Chpt. 9	• Striker v goalkeeper • 1 v 1 + goalkeeper • All positional games in direction of goal (situations of numerical superiority)	• Attack v defense • Games with smaller and larger teams

Basic techniques in the "preliminary" phase

The young beginners must get used to the way the ball behaves. They do this by coming into contact with the ball as often as possible so that they can experience how the ball reacts. Gradually they slowly develop a feel for the ball, learn how hard they need to kick it, how to kick it in a given direction, how to kick it through the air, how to keep in contact with it while running at speed, etc.

These are the initial steps towards developing soccer technique. We have therefore designed a practice drill which is highly suitable for developing a feel for the ball in young players. The following description of the "city game" illustrates how the youngest player's play can be shaped during coaching. The playing area should measure about 30 yards square, and a smaller square measuring 5 x 5 or 6 x 6 yards should be marked off in each corner.

Each of these smaller squares is assigned the name of a city, e.g. Groningen, Maastricht, Amsterdam and Den Haag; choosing the names of towns in the vicinity of the club is also a popular option.

Give each player a ball and distribute the players over the four cities. You then have a structure which offers a lot of options for realizing your aim: fostering a feel for the ball in your pupils.

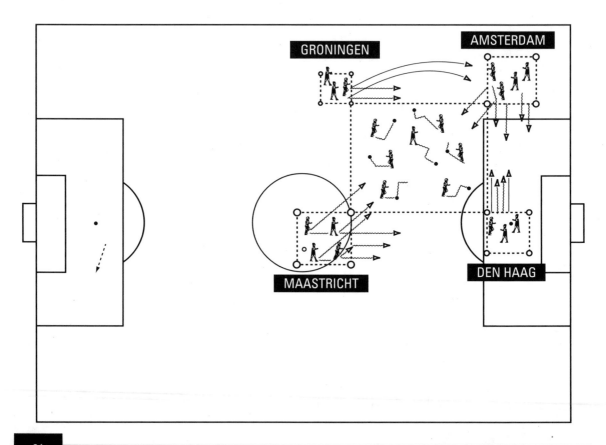

How to play the city game

You can tell your players to travel around the country by any route you wish. Obviously the choice is yours, but we want to take this opportunity to give a few examples below.

1. The players push the ball "along the road" from city to city, in a direction which you have previously specified, until they arrive back in their "home" city.

- You can ask the players to travel slowly ("move like a tricycle") or faster ("move like a race car").

- At a later stage you can let the players choose their own route. You will have to make it clear to them that they have to use the roads and be careful not to collide with each other.

- You can introduce a little variety by asking the players to touch the ball as few or as many times as possible between two cities. In the first case the players develop a feeling for distance and in the second they learn how to keep the ball as close as possible to their feet.

- You can take things further by asking the players to try to send the ball to the next city with a single kick. Obviously they should not all take the same route, but don't forget to say so when you actually do this!

You can combine the above variations at will. Always remember that what seems like a minor variation to an adult may be a total novelty for a child of six.

The full potential of the city game is far from exhausted, because so far we have only used the "roads".

"Who will get to Amsterdam first?"

2. If you decide to use the area between the "roads", i.e. the center section of the whole playing area (the "water"), you will have a lot more options.

- You can use the diagonals. For example: the players can travel around the country at will, from city to city, by road and by water. On the roads they can take it easy, but if they go by water they have to hurry, because the boat is sinking. Obviously you can come up with another story to introduce some other variation.

- All the players swim through the water and take care not to bump into each other. When you give a sign they all have to swim back to their own city as fast as possible.

- All the players set off at the same time to swim to the next city. Who can swim fastest?

- A few players swim in the water, but without a ball. The other are all in their own cities, and try to travel over the roads to the other cities. The swimmers try to tag the travelers. You can use a system of awarding points, or you can let the players change roles after a tag.

The city game offers a number of other options as the players progress:

- You can use a different interpretation of the playing area.
  You can change the city game into a country game. This may not seem much of   a change to an adult, but this is not how players see it. You could go further and make a castle with four towers from the playing area. This gives you lots of opportunity for thinking up new stories and ways of playing with the ball.

- You can change the structure of the playing area. You may want to make the playing area larger, e.g. 45 x 45 yards, for second-year players. This gives you a bigger infield square. When you use the city or country game, with the paths and the water, what's to stop you creating an island in the middle of the water? A treasure island, for instance. This just asks for a story with pirates, and so on.

At this age parents still have to help in the dressing room.

- You can use scoring systems more easily than with the first year players
  You might have noticed that we have only touched lightly on the subject of scoring. Of course, scoring is also

The Hague Tower	The Road		Amsterdam Tower Netherlands
The Road	Water Courtyard	Water Courtyard Treasure Island where the Castle's inhabitants live Water Courtyard	The Road
Maastricht Tower England	The Road		Groningen Tower Germany

important for "first years" (scoring is always a key element of soccer), but players of 6 and 7 are not yet focused on comparing and competing. Players of 8 and 9 are usually more competitive, and this can be exploited by assigning points for the various components of the city game.

Naturally you can think up your own competitive variations for incorporation in the city game.

As you see, the basic structure of the city game gives you all sorts of different options for working with young soccer players. This will also be true of other related games and structures which you yourself can devise, and there is no reason why you should not do so.

To repeat our initial premise: the aim of the coach must be to develop a feel for the ball in his young charges, and to improve their ball control in soccer situations. They should therefore all have a ball, and spend as much time with the ball as possible.

All sorts of basic technical skills such as dribbling, pushing the ball forward, receiving and passing the ball, and also shooting, can be dealt with in the city game. And these basic skills will undoubtedly be present in any variations of these games which you yourself devise.

We know that there is a great temptation to let your pupils practice each of these technical skills separately.

We have no objection to this, provided it is done as a worthwhile variation between the games and competitive games.

1. Clearly demonstrate what is required, especially in the case of the first year players. At their age they have an excellent talent for imitation. It is also necessary to talk through the demonstration, but it is most important that you show the players how to carry out the movements. The children must be able to form a picture of what they have to do, and how they have to do it. The aim of the exercise must be clear (try to be fastest to the other side, touch the ball the most times, etc.).

2. In the course of playing a small sided game, it is OK to stop the game and practice a basic skill separately if the inability to perform the skill is interfering with the object of the game. Do not ask the players to carry out two or more exercises for different skills in sequence. It is better to concentrate on one skill and allow the players to occupy themselves with it for a while, before then continuing with the small sided game.

3. Players of 6 usually have little or no control of the direction of the ball. In their case the ball must be the only obstacle. You can give second-year players more obstacles to deal with, e.g. by asking them to play the ball through "gates" (the width and distance will depend on the abilities of the players) or into the corners of a full-size goal (use cones as markers).

And those who follow a coaching course can learn how to apply it in reality.

Basic techniques and homework

As has already been mentioned, the youngest players (from 6 years old) are hardly able to kick a ball. The ball is a major obstacle or difficulty factor for them. First of all, therefore, they must familiarize themselves with the ball. They can do this in the course of simple games played with a light ball, a rubber ball, a foam-rubber ball or a volleyball ball. The objective is to get a feel for the ball, for catching it, throwing it, stopping it and kicking it.

When they have played soccer for a little longer, from about age 7, they can start to learn properly by playing games. This demands the use of basic techniques such as pushing the ball forward, dribbling, and the various means of retaining the ball. Passing and kicking steadily improve, and the youngsters learn not to be frightened to head the ball. By the time they are 11, youngsters are quite skillful in juggling the ball and keeping it in the air.

The emphasis during training sessions with the youngest players will be on developing their technique, but one or two hours each week are not enough to acquire good technical skills. More time is needed. Rinus Michels has spoken about this: "When kids used to play soccer in the streets they played all day and every day. They couldn't get enough of it. A ball, a goal made from a couple of coats, trees, drains or walls, and a clear section of street was all they needed. If there was no one to play with, you practiced your kicking technique in order to avoid becoming bored. You mastered the game just by playing, without any intervention by adults. Some proved better than others: after all, mother nature has her whims and moods. But you learned. Without thinking about it, you did nothing other than endlessly repeat different activities with the ball until the ball became an extension of yourself, even a means of expressing yourself." Learning to control the ball still demands a great deal of time.

Concentration on performing the technique.

This time is not available within a club context. Aspiring soccer players therefore have to do a lot of practicing in their free time. Coaches must kindle the enthusiasm of their charges so that they devote more hours to playing, as a sort of "homework". Technique can be improved in various ways during training sessions and unsupervised homework. A number of options are described below.

Coerver-School

Wiel Coerver is an especially enthusiastic coach, who has studied the technique of the world's best soccer players and made it the basis of his soccer coaching system. Coerver has written his books from the point of view that a soccer player's technique is the basic measure of his value for his team and his teammates. He believes that a player who masters all the movements which are described in his books will be able to come out on top in almost every soccer situation.

The Dutch Soccer Association does not share this belief. Wiel Coerver focuses solely on the mechanics of the various movements and equates these with playing soccer itself. He ignores all the other difficulty factors/obstacles which a player has to overcome if he is to perform ever more successfully in competitive soccer. Stars such as Romario and Bergkamp have a lot more soccer talents than just good technique. Wiel Coerver has focused on just one - admittedly very important - soccer obstacle and based his coaching system on that one aspect, technique.

In short, Coerver says that players can best learn to play soccer by learning certain movements with the ball. The Dutch Soccer Association says that players can best learn to play soccer by playing soccer. A soccer match demands much more from the players than just technical skills. Insight and communication are key aspects of playing soccer. However, this certainly does not mean that Coerver's system is of no value.

Technique is important for a soccer player, and it has been found in practice that the use of Coerver's coaching material to achieve the objective of teaching good movement technique with the ball can yield good results. This is why the Dutch Soccer Association is happy to use the "Coerver method" to make a contribution to the individual development of young players.

As with all components of soccer coaching, of course, it is important that the players have a positive attitude towards it. It must be experienced as enjoyable, because this is the most important precondition for being able to achieve anything. In general terms, the coaching material can be used as follows.

The youngest players also need a sweatsuit jacket during the warm-up.

1. As part of the warming-up

If you do this, you must pay attention to two things: only use an organization, and moves which the players have already practiced (there is then no need for the players to stand still while the move is demonstrated). Utilize the moves preferably at the end of the warming-up, when the players' are not so stiff.

2. As active rest during a training session

During training sessions for young soccer players we try to ensure that the players never have to stand around idle, with nothing to do. On the other hand we sometimes insert a short rest period between two strenuous exercises. Such rest periods can be used, provided the situation allows this and the players are not too exhausted, to practice some of the "repertoire" of the Coerver

system. The pause between two small sided or competitive games can also be used for this.

3. As homework

Many players like to play soccer outside the hours of their club matches and training sessions. They may do this with friends or alone, after school on a local field, or on a Saturday or Sunday afternoon while other games are being played, or during school breaks, on free afternoons, during vacations, etc.

Sometimes they will play a game, but they may simply kick a ball "aimlessly" around. At such moments it would obviously be worthwhile for them to practice some of the movements of the Coerver system. It cannot do any harm to encourage youngsters to practice the movements as a sort of voluntary homework.

4. During soccer camps, etc.

By soccer camps we mean not only the camp weeks which are organized by the Dutch Soccer Association but also the camps and mini-camps which are organized by the clubs themselves. On these occasions there is usually so much time reserved for soccer coaching that it can be worthwhile to devote some of it to Coerver's exercises.

Lots of practice makes perfect.

Just two final comments on the Coerver method.

- The use of his practice exercises is only worthwhile if the players involved have already achieved a reasonable level of technical skill.

There is little point in encouraging players to practice movements to beat an opponent when they cannot yet kick the ball properly.

- Players are not puppets! When they carry out the exercises, they need to know the practical purpose of these movements. Never make them perform a movement simply in response to a given signal. Make sure that the movement has a purpose, e.g. a feint and a 90° turn are of practical use if another player wants to run into space and needs a change of direction to facilitate this.

Soccer tennis

Soccer tennis differs from the already described basic games. Nevertheless, many top soccer players are very familiar with soccer tennis. This is an ideal game for demonstrating your technique: heading, juggling, controlling the ball, and playing it through the air. It is also great fun. Many top coaches put a high priority on soccer tennis: during more serious training sessions in a training camp before the season starts or after it finishes.

Soccer tennis creates good team spirit and is eminently suitable for improving and maintaining technique. Not only top players but also college and youth players can enjoy it. It can be played with a net, but a stretched cord also suffices.

The rules are as shown below. However, some care is required, because they have to be adapted to the level and age of the players.

Players in the 8 to 10 age group can play too, but they must be able to touch the ball as often as they want. The server holds the ball in his hands before letting it fall and volleying it over the net. The ball can be allowed to bounce a number of times.

In short, players and coaches themselves can agree on the modifications to the rules. The guiding principle should be: to keep the game flowing as long as possible without interruption. Soccer tennis is also an ideal game for the gymnasium.

How is soccer tennis played?

1. The game is played between 2 teams of 3 or 4 players.

2. The game is started by volleying the ball over the net from behind the serving team's base line.

3. The service must pass over the net in such a way that it would land between the net and the opponents' base line.

4. Only the serving team can score points.

5. 1 or 2 points can be scored during each service sequence by heading or kicking the ball.

6. A "score" by the receiving team causes it to become the serving team.

7. A set is won by scoring 15 points, provided the difference to the opposing team's score is at least 2 points. If this is not the case, the set is continued until the margin of 2 points is achieved.

8a. The match is won by winning two sets. The teams change ends after each set.

8b. A time limit is set.

The most important aspect is that the coach can take any necessary measures to facilitate the flow of the game.
Different rules apply for younger and older players.
Different rules apply for skillful and less skillful players.

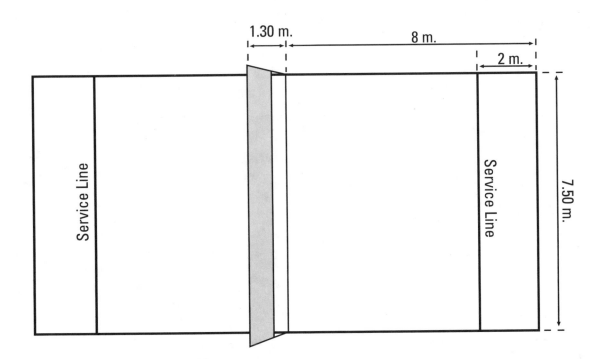

Be bold. Change the rules from game to game. What matters is winning, not what rules are applied.

Examples and modifications

- Point can/cannot be scored directly from the service
- First ball can/cannot be caught
- Allow ball to bounce 3 times per player/ per team

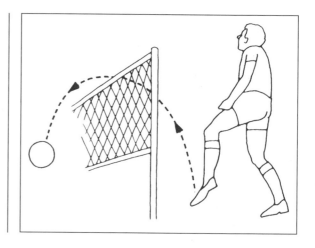

Soccer tennis can be played wherever there is a net. Naturally shirts must be worn during training sessions and tournaments.

CHAPTER 8

4 AGAINST 4:
BETTER SOCCER, MORE FUN!

What is 4 against 4?

Playing soccer

Four against four (usually referred to as 4 v 4) embodies the key elements in the process of learning to play soccer: "Soccer is best learned by playing soccer".

Obviously there is only a small chance of mastering the game and developing skills in games involving teams of 11 against 11. The situation is too complex for beginners, there is little opportunity for playing a full role in such games, and the average number of ball contacts is too low. In short, there are too few opportunities for genuinely participating in the game.

"Well kept in!"

Coaching

We might want 7-year-olds to exploit the available space properly and try to win the ball back at just the right moment, but in practice these demands are much too difficult for players of this age.

Players should not be exposed to over-ambitious or excessively high expectations. In general the emphasis of coaching should conform to the following pattern at the various stages of the player's progress. 4 v 4 (or derivations of it) is an ideal framework for teaching these various elements.

Beginners

* Explanations and demonstrations of technique (how to pass, dribble, receive the ball, control it, etc.).

* Controlling the ball. The emphasis must be on mastering the ball.

* The structure and rules of the game, the dimensions of the pitch and the size of the goals must facilitate the acquisition of technical skills, i.e. mastery of the ball.

* Besides ball control, other obstacles must be gradually introduced into the learning process (goal-orientedness, reduced space, less time, more opponents, more difficult situations through a larger number of players).

Before children can play the game they must learn to kick, stop and dribble the ball, at however elementary a level. They will therefore have to be given instruction in these basic skills.

Juniors

- Besides instruction at the technical level, which will always have to be given when the situation requires it, the coach will have to deal with the subject of insight into the objectives of the game.

- The players' ball control will have improved (some players will have developed faster than others) and attention must now be focused on applying the acquired technical skills to facilitate the objectives of the game.

- The so-called insight aspects of the game must be developed methodically (in a logical sequence) and systematically (what comes first, what follows, and what comes later).

- In this phase it is important that the players appreciate that the objective of playing soccer is to win the game, and that this requires a certain individual and collective attitude. The tasks within the team will have to be explained clearly.

- The ability to read a game has to be developed. Players must learn to recognize soccer situations and to interpret and assess them on the basis of their experience, so that they can make correct decisions.

At this stage the players, even though they are of the same age, still differ considerably in their play and appearance. This is largely a consequence of differences in aptitude and talent, but may also reflect contrasting attitudes to the game. There are wide differences in skill, interest, concentration, discipline, reactions, etc.

The coach helps to foster insight into the game.

In practice this an everyday reality, and therefore an everyday problem, for coaches.

The details of coaching 4 v 4 are given in Chapter 6 under the basic games.

Summary

Games of 4 v 4 contain all the elements that make street soccer so attractive. They are competitive, each player has a lot of ball contacts, and lots of goals can be scored. In short, all the aims of a soccer game come to the fore.

This easily organized game brings lots of pleasure to both young and old. And 4 v 4 is highly suitable for teaching players to play soccer - more so than 3 v 3 or 5 v 5.

Innumerable soccer problems have to be solved. And none of the players can hold back, because this would disadvantage his 3 teammates enormously.

For the players, 4 v 4 is an objective in itself. They want to win, and they want to play as well as possible. Coaches must however view the game as a means to an end.

It must not be regarded as an additional way of gaining laurels for the club. That is what genuine competitive matches are there for!

Tussle for the ball.

What 4 v 4 is not

In recent years 4 v 4 has sometimes become an objective in itself rather than a means to an end. This is usually the result of a lack of qualified supervision. In such cases 4 v 4 becomes an instrument with which clubs, coaches or parents try, cost what it may, to gain prestige. This is nothing more nor less than the exploitation of children to satisfy their elders' thirst for success.

4 v 4 is not intended to be another competitive element alongside existing club competitions (7 v 7 for players aged

6 to 10, and 11 v 11 for older players). The weekly match against another club must remain the highlight of the week.

All the work, practice and coaching is focused on the weekly game. In this context a game of 4 v 4 is simply a means to an end. If the 4 v 4 game is only used to fight soccer battles at full tilt, then it is not fulfilling its purpose. Its purpose is to provide a simple framework within which a coach can focus on typical soccer situations in order for the players to learn the elements of the game.

The pace of a player's soccer development should not be forced. Players should be able to concentrate on their own play. Within the restraints of the small number of players and the small playing area, there are sufficient opportunities for them to shine and to learn to recognize certain situations themselves and come up with solutions to the problems involved.

The role of the coach should be to point out how the player's own solutions can be improved or modified, rather than to force the players into a straitjacket or regard them as puppets in his own game, his struggle for success.

The 4 v 4 game is played by and for children. The role of adults in the street soccer of former years was restricted to confiscating the ball when the flowers in his yard were flattened for the umpteenth time (this, of course, also encouraged the development of technical skills).

If an adult, coach, instructor, father or mother lacks the necessary soccer background to recognize critical soccer situations and comment sensibly on them, he or she should remain in the background and simply observe the game as a spectator.

If such an adult should want to become involved, then the best thing to do is to follow a course in which the role of a coach is explained in a systematic and methodical way.

The Dutch Soccer Association organizes courses for youth coaches and managers to help adults who want to work with young soccer players.

A good coach will look at a player's development (age, aptitude, motivation) and use 4 v 4 as a means of introducing the player to certain aspects of "real" soccer matches (7 v 7 or 11 v 11). Such a coach will also be able to exploit all kinds of derived forms of 4 v 4 in order to achieve certain teaching objectives.

A coach must be able to translate frequently occurring situations in "real" games of soccer into comparable situations in 4 v 4. He certainly should not restrict himself to pushing his charges to win a 4 v 4 game at all costs. It is simply not important enough. Certainly for adults.

Why 4 v 4?

The choice of 4 v 4 is arbitrary, but it does conceal a worthy purpose.

At the basis of the modern method of teaching players the fundamentals of the game is the decision to choose a number of basic games as a framework which guarantees that the players will always be playing soccer. The promotion and realization of this concept required the creation of a symbol to make the content of this concept clear.

A small sided game is the most suitable vehicle for this concept. It includes all the elements which soccer can offer: Technical and physical skills, Insight into the game, and Communication with teammates and opponents: in short, TIC (see Chapter 1).

It was felt that 4 v 4 comes closest to the basic characteristics of a real match. 4 v 4 contains the most important characteristics of the game of soccer.

The small number of players (4) encourages the use of the depth and width of the playing area as required. A square pass can be assigned a function by making a forward pass conditional on a prior square pass. Or a forward pass can be played and the subsequent threat of a square or return pass can pull an opponent out of position. Here too the square pass has a clear function and is typical of competitive situations.

4 v 4 is the smallest manifestation of a real match

Square passes followed by a forward pass, and a forward pass followed by a square or return pass, are functional and typical of real matches. It is true that such situations also arise in games involving other numbers of players, e.g. 5 v 5 or 3 v 3, but in 3 v 3 they occur less often.

The number of players defines the structure of the game. With 3 players there are less opportunities to exploit the function of the square pass as a condition for a forward pass, and thus less opportunities for learning. There is one less direction for distributing the ball, the 3 v 3 game could be the next step in the sequence following the 1 v 1 duel.

In 4 v 4 by contrast, there are options in all directions of play. In 5 v 5 the situation is different to that which prevails in 3 v 3. However, because there are 2 more players on the field, the forward pass and the function of the square pass are less clear (certainly from a coaching and teaching viewpoint). Many situations arise in which several players play the same role and get in each other's way. The play then appears chaotic and uncontrolled (without structure).

It cannot be said that small sided games other than 4 v 4 would have no effect. On the contrary.

If a coach identifies specific elements associated with a small sided game, it is sensible to use such games with proper coaching.

Attack and defensive situations occur frequently and inseparably in 4 v 4.

This is also the case with other games than those referred to. This subject is dealt with in more detail in the Chapter "Didactics and Methods".

4 v 4 is the smallest manifestation of a real match. So many comparable situations occur in such a short period of time that players learn to solve these problems very flexibly.

No two situations are identical (time, timing, speed, direction, etc. are always different). However, the structure and the aim are always the same.

Flexibility is an important aspect of soccer training. This is in contrast to other branches of sport, where each movement has to be precisely the same each time it is carried out (e.g. gymnastics). Great importance therefore attaches to being able to "read" soccer situations.

Being able to recognize constantly recurring situations when one or the other team has the ball is an important precondition for taking the correct action and applying the required technical skill (ball control, ball speed, direction of pass, challenging for the ball at the right moment).

A game of 4 v 4 (and all similar and derived games) generates lots of situations, involves all the players (even if some of them get in the way) and guarantees lots of repetition. Above all it is a game, and youngsters love games, don't they?

Lots of recognizable situations occur in 4 v 4.

The rules of 4 v 4

Whether they are young beginners or more advanced juniors, youth players need clear rules.

4 v 4 therefore has a number of rules which are intended to safeguard the objectives of the game. The game must be played in such a way that it flows.

An example: If each goal is so small that one player can completely guard it, then it becomes impossible to achieve one of the objectives of the game when in possession, namely scoring goals. In such a situation the rules must be amended. The goals must be enlarged until they offer a reasonable chance of scoring.

A number of variations on the basic game of 4 v 4 are also described, in which modifications of the structure and or rules of the game enable the players to try to achieve other objectives.

Irrespective of the structure and rules which apply, it is important to implement the rules strictly.

When the ball goes out of play, for instance, the opposing team is given a kick-in. Defensive fouls must be punished by a free-kick (point out how the situation could have been solved better).

Before the game starts the coach should explain the objectives of the game and describe the rules (brief and to the point - no long-winded explanations). It is very important that he pays attention to whether the players carry out their tasks as agreed (in respect of the objectives and the rules). All coaches should be aware that the application of the rules is a very important means of influencing the course of the game.

Actions such as shielding the ball, or beating an opponent with the ball, can be encouraged by introducing certain rules.

The coach must focus on the situations that he wants to instruct on (for example: pressuring the ball after losing possession). He must remain alert for the right moment to give instructions, and demonstrate what he wants to get across.

It is beneficial - certainly in games of 4 v 4 - to apply a minimal number of rules. Rules promote the flow of the game and give the players a clear idea of how the game is to be played. And if the players are clear about what they are doing, this increases the returns from the practice time and playing time.

The principle on which the rules are based is that the players must spend as much time as possible playing. This means that there is no time wasted on many of the things that may be necessary in a game of 11 v 11, but are not really relevant to the aims of 4 v 4. Stoppages must be as short as possible. In practice this means:

Starting the game

- The kick-off is in the middle of the field.

- After a goal is scored, the game is resumed by dribbling the ball into play from the goal.

Ball goes out of play

- Kick-in instead of throw-in, because this is quicker and there is no need to wait

The pitch must be marked out.

until teammates have found space (for older players a specific choice can be made for throw-ins in order to learn about throwing in and its associated aspects such as timing, taking up position, feinting, etc.).

The youngest players are usually not capable of dealing with a thrown-in ball, and this would lead to interruptions in the flow of the game, thus defeating the aim of the exercise: to play as much as possible.

- When a kick-in is taken the opponents must be at least 3 yards from the ball.

Ball goes over the goal line

- The ball is played in from the goal line (dribbled in or kicked).

Offside

- No offside rule in this basic game. However, it can be useful with older juniors or adults.

Corners

- Teach players to take short corners with opponents at least 3 yards from the ball. Resume positional play as soon as possible: no high balls in front of such a small goal from such a short distance.

Free-kicks

- Offenses such as dirty play, foul tackles and hands are punished with a indirect free- kick; the opponents must stand at least 3 yards from the ball. Tapped free-kicks are therefore possible, so that positional play can be quickly resumed.

- Preventing a goal by handling the ball is punished by a penalty kick. Distance from goal: 15 yards; no goalkeeper. Encourage players not to linger in front of goal: "If you haven't got the ball you can't score, so try to win the ball!".

- **Note**: Let the players be their own referee, then you can concentrate on the play. The coach is the coach!

How the coach can modify the rules

- If the play doesn't flow, the coach can implement the following measures at restart situations:
  - first ball is free
  - dribbling in is allowed.

The ability to hold the ball is one of the first requirements for an attacker.

In 4 v 4 the rules are never rigid. There is no umbrella organization such as FIFA to lay down strict rules for the game.

The main thing is that coaches, on the basis of their insight into the players under their charge (age, talent, motivation, insight into the game), choose the right rules for the game. The coach must be able to apply the right rules in order to get the best out of the game.

An example: The players are not good at regaining the ball, and increasingly tend to stay together in front of the goal.

The coach could widen or heighten the goal in order to force the players to defend their goal by getting closer to the ball and thus preventing their opponents from shooting. He will have to encourage this by means of his coaching, and try to improve his players insight into "why".

He can also try to achieve this by telling his players to imagine that there is only one minute to play in an important match, and that extra-time will have to be played if a goal is scored.

In this case he tries to achieve his objectives by setting a task and by means of jointly agreed rules which appeal to the players' imagination and stimulate certain behavior (winning the ball).

If a game of 4 v 4 is played in the context of a club tournament or a divisional championship, the rules must be explained clearly beforehand to all concerned.

In such cases 4 v 4 is less a means of practicing and more an attractive form of club activity. The aim is therefore to achieve the best possible result.

Certainly it is desired for players to have a winner mentality, although only within the existing rules which have been specified for the occasion.

Learning to get to grips with rules is also a very important teaching aim in soccer. Coaches and managers should agree to take a more distanced approach to winning such championships and competitions. They should be able to realize the purpose of such events.

The coach defines the scenario, and only the affected players are involved in the action.

The contents of 4 v 4:

Every person who watches a soccer game notices different things. One person might notice the dominant player with the ball, another person might observe a player make the same technical mistakes when he kicks the ball, and a third person only notices the physical capabilities of the players.

When you look at a 4 v 4 game through the eyes of a coach who is interested in improving the performance of the players, you need to know the structure or method through which you can receive relevant information to base your coaching on.

The tasks of a coach during 4 v 4:

A. Know what the objectives are in soccer.
B. Have knowledge and insight in the technical requirements needed to play the game(how to receive, pass, head, dribble, shoot a ball, see chapter 7).
C. Make the correct coaching remarks, give the right examples, choose the correct training activities, with in mind what the players need/want to learn (have to possess knowledge of the development stages in youngsters).

Variation of the basic 4 v 4 form:

Earlier on, we discussed that the 4 v 4 game is not the only training activity which aids in the learning process. Players first need to master the basic technical skills. In other words they have to be the master over the ball, and not the other way around. This is the first step which needs to be accomplished before the youngsters can play the game. As soon as children have a feel for the ball, (can dribble, kick, stop, and control the ball at an elementary skill level) they need to begin refining these skills in basic games like 4 v 4. Soccer is more than mastering the ball, the technical skills should never become an objective in itself.

To learn to play the game there are several additional elements to be conquered. The ball is only the means with which the objectives of the game must be realized. Through the several basic games, the objectives of soccer will be realized. Every basic game has its own difficulties/obstacles which have to be mastered.

For example in 1 v 1, the specific difficulty is to get passed the opponent with the ball (obstacles are: the ball, the opponent, and getting to the goalline) In the basic form of 5 v 2 in a rectangle, the difficulty is to keep possession of the ball under pressure of the opponents (obstacles are: the ball, opponents, and the limited space). The realization of the objectives of soccer, or in other words: to get the result, yield, effect, while playing soccer, the technical skills are very

Even the youngest beginners use technique as a means to an end.

important, but just as important are the insight in the game, and the communication (verbal and non-verbal) between the players. (TIC) As mentioned earlier with young players the emphasis should be on the development of the technical skills, and older more advanced players need to learn insight in the game.

This has to be clearly visible during the coaching while doing the different basic games. <u>The important quality of the basic games is that the players are always playing soccer.</u> The training, therefore, has the right ingredients for a positive learning environment (competitiveness, excitement, intrinsic motivation).

In the variations of 4 v 4 which will be explained later in this chapter, the game is tweeked just enough to realize different objectives. The different rules, dimensions of the field and goals, organization, and assignment within the game changes the look of the game. This different look in itself changes the demands which are placed on the players, which makes it possible to have different learning moments. These demands could be within the technical, the physical, mental, or the communication and cooperation aspect of the game. It is up to the coach to recognize the specific character of each variation, and to coach the players within the learning moments of that basic game. In the modern game of soccer the <u>goalkeepers</u> role has gotten bigger. These 4 v 4 basic games are extremely suitable to develop the soccer playing qualities of each and every player, including the goalkeeper.

Dutch internationals also play daily small-sided games to help them improve.

The ingredients of 4 v 4

The objectives of the game (in the context of the 3 main moments)

1. In possession

A team in possession close to its own goal aims to initiate its buildup play.
- The main aspects are organization and taking up the right positions at the correct distances from each other (balance).
- Good positional play, with the aim of keeping possession of the ball, and passing it forward or deep into the opposition's half.

2. Opponents in possession

A player in possession near the opposition's goal aims to create a scoring opportunity or to score himself.

If the ball is at a safe distance from the defending team's goal, the aim is to disrupt the opposition's buildup play.
- Above all, try not to be beaten.
- Play close to each other (compact).
- Pressure the opposition.

Close to the defending team's goal the first aim is to prevent the opposition from scoring and the second aim is to regain the ball.
- Shield the goal properly and (if necessary) cover teammates' backs.
- Keep opponent and ball in front of you.
- Blocking shots (block tackle, etc.).
- Win the ball.
- Don't foul.

3. Change of possession (transition)

Adapt immediately to the new situation in thought and deed.

Players' tasks in 4 v 4

The sweeper

OWN TEAM IN POSSESSION

KEY TO SYMBOLS

→ Pass (path of the ball)

〜〜► Player dribbles

--- ► Player makes a run

▬▬▬ = own team possession

▬▬▬ = opponents in possession

Black shirts =
        Team A (in possession)
White shirts =
        Team B (not in possession)

Objectives
- Start the buildup
- Launch an attack and ultimately try to score

Required skills, knowledge, response
T.I.C.
Technique:
- Passing and kicking (short/long)
- Receiving and controlling the ball
- Dribbling
- Shielding the ball

Insight:
- Correct positioning (central, sideways to the left and right flanks, forwards and backwards)
- Direction of play
- Always be ready to play the ball forward
- Avoid losing the ball - take no risks
- Passing square is often a means of creating an opportunity to play a forward pass
- Make backpass possible.

Communication:
- Reading the play
- Recognizing situations
- Correct ball speed
- Right moment to ask for ball/ move into space
- Instruct teammates on situation, opponents' play
- Encourage attack

Players' tasks in 4 v 4

The sweeper

OPPONENTS IN POSSESSION

KEY TO SYMBOLS

→ Pass (path of the ball)
〰▶ Player dribbles
- - -▶ Player makes a run

▬▬▬ = own team possession

▬▬▬ = opponents in possession

Black shirts =
    Team A (in possession)
White shirts =
    Team B (not in possession)

Objectives
- Avoid conceding a goal
- Nullify opponents' striker
- Win the ball

Required skills, knowledge, response
T.I.C.
Technique:
- Follow opponent
- Forechecking
- Blocking tackle, sliding tackle
- Defensive headers

Insight:
- Tight marking
- Look beyond immediate opponent, read the situation further away
- Don't be beaten
- Cover teammates' backs, don't be pulled too far out of the center, always screen the goal
- Take over the most dangerous opposing player (takes precedence over direct opponent)

Communication:
- Instruct players in own team
- Encourage teammates

Players' tasks in 4 v 4

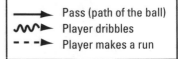

KEY TO SYMBOLS

→ Pass (path of the ball)
〰► Player dribbles
- - -► Player makes a run

▬▬▬ = own team possession

▬▬▬ = opponents in possession

Black shirts =
    Team A (in possession)
White shirts =
    Team B (not in possession)

Objectives
- Carry on the buildup (positional game) in order to set up an attack (scoring opportunities)

Required skills, knowledge, response
T.I.C.

Technique:
- Passing and kicking (short/long)
- Receiving and controlling the ball
- Dribbling, individual run
- Shooting at goal
- Heading at goal
- Shielding the ball

Insight:
- Correct positioning (use space to best effect, distance to teammates)
- Avoid losing the ball unnecessarily - take no risks
- Play yourself free (run, 1-2 combination, ball takeover)
- Goal-orientedness (turn up in front of goal)
- Make backpass possible.

Communication:
- Ask for the ball (with or without prior dummy run)
- Correct ball speed
- Instruct forward players ("man on", "time", "pass", "turn right", "go yourself", etc.)

Players' tasks in 4 v 4

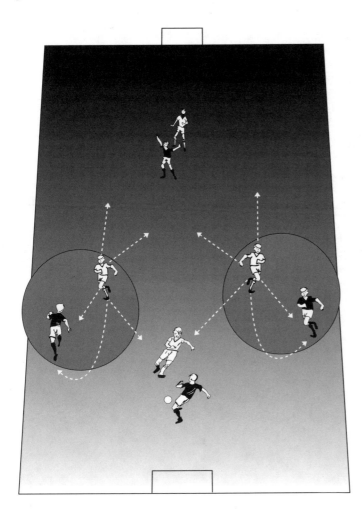

Midfielders

OPPONENTS IN POSSESSION

Objectives
- Disrupt opponents' buildup
- Defend against opponent's attack
- Win the ball
- Screen space behind
- Prevent goal, stop most dangerous opponent

Required skills, knowledge, response
T.I.C.
Technique:
- Screen opponent
- Effective runs (keep knees bent)
- Win the ball (sliding tackle, feint to challenge)
- Agility, speed of reaction

Insight:
- Correct positioning (forwards, backwards, inwards - "squeeze" - outwards)
- Give cover
- Mark direct opponent
- Cut off the option of a forward pass
- Take over the most dangerous opposing player
- Don't be beaten
- Play close to each other, compactly
- Box in the opponent (cut off backpass)

Communication:
- Instruct each other, certainly most forward player
- Anticipate defensive actions by most forward player (e.g. force into a corner)

Players' tasks in 4 v 4

Forward

OWN TEAM IN POSSESSION

KEY TO SYMBOLS

➡️	Pass (path of the ball)
〰️➤	Player dribbles
┄┄➤	Player makes a run

▬▬▬ = own team possession

▬▬▬ = opponents in possession

Black shirts =
       Team A (in possession)
White shirts =
       Team B (not in possession)

Objectives
- Attacking and scoring

Required skills, knowledge, response
T.I.C.
Technique:
- Receiving the ball and finding space
- Dummy runs
- Beating an opponent
- Finishing: shooting, heading, chipping, lobbing
- Laying the ball off
- Shielding the ball
- Passing

Insight:
- Keep space open, make space
- Buildup with other players. Good anticipation.
- Ask for ball at the right moment
- Hold the ball
- Make space for advancing midfielder on the flank (stay clear)
- Goal-orientedness

Communication:
- Ask for the ball
- Dummy runs
- Make yourself visible (in the final third, move towards the ball)

Players' tasks in 4 v 4

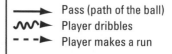

KEY TO SYMBOLS

→ Pass (path of the ball)
〰► Player dribbles
- - -► Player makes a run

▬▬▬ = own team possession

▬▬▬ = opponents in possession

Black shirts =
        Team A (in possession)
White shirts =
        Team B (not in possession)

Objectives

- Disrupt opponents' buildup
- Prevent long ball forward
- Gain time so that teammates can recover/regroup
- Force opponents to buildup on a given side of the field

Required skills, knowledge, response
T.I.C.
Technique:

- Screen space behind you
- Effective runs (keep knees bent)
- Win the ball (possibly feint to challenge first)
- Sliding tackle. Do not foul!!!

Insight:

- Force square pass, cut off option of forward ball
- Force opponent to the flank, box him in, don't let him escape
- Pressure the player with the ball
- Choose right moment to challenge for the ball (instructions from behind)
- Drop back closer to teammates (do not allow yourself to be beaten)

Communication:

- "Read" the intentions of the player with the ball
- Maintain contact with other players
- Make (dummy) runs to indicate where and when the ball can be won

Variants of 4 v 4

Basic game 4 v 4

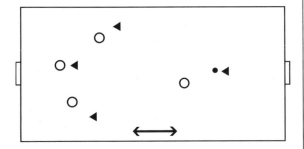

Dimensions, depending on age and level of skill:
  length: 44 yards
  width: 22 yards
  goals: at least 3.5 yards wide

4 v 4 with 4 small goals

Modified rules:
- Goals can be scored in 2 small goals.

Characteristics
Own side in possession:
- Scoring chances can be created by switching rapidly from one part of the field to another.

Opponents in possession:
- Defend well by means of positional play.
- Force opponent to play square.
- Regain the ball.

Demands on the game:
Own side in possession:
- Keep the ball moving very quickly.
- 1-touch or 2-touch play.
- Good positional play.
- Recognize the right moment to ask for the ball.

Rinus Michels and Dick Advocaat devote a lot of time studying how youngsters learn to play soccer.

Opponents in possession:
- Well organized (positional play).
- Recognize the right moment to try to win the ball.
- Defend actively (disrupt opponents' buildup).

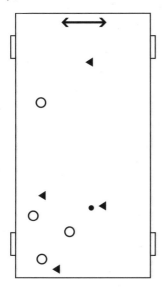

Dimensions, depending on age and level of skill:
   length: 17 - 20 yards
   width: 44 yards

Technical skills needed for this game:

Passing with the inside of the foot

Why the inside of the foot?
- Accuracy
- Fast, short play (positional play)

Focusing points for the technical execution
- Choose a good position relative to the ball (be aware).
- Supporting leg:
  Slightly bent, close to the ball, with foot usually pointing in direction of play.
- Kicking leg:
  Turned slightly outwards, knee and ankle bent.
- Kicking foot:
  Turned slightly outwards, at right angles to direction of play, tip of foot raised, ankle taut.
- Area of contact:
  Hit the ball with the inside of the foot:
- If the point of contact is low, the ball flies high.
- If the point of contact is high, the ball stays low.

Receiving and controlling the ball

Why should a player receive and control the ball?
- The ball cannot be played to another player with just one touch.
- The play has to be switched from a crowded area to a more open area.

Focusing points for the technical execution
- Choose a good position relative to the ball and the opposing players (be aware).
- The ball can be received and controlled with all parts of the body except the arms and hands (instep, inside of the foot, sole of foot, thigh, chest/abdomen, head).
- Principle: first move towards the ball then, just like a hanging net, cushion the ball supply and flexibly, thus "killing" and controlling it.
- Maintain balance through positioning of arms.
- Use as few actions as possible to make the ball playable.
- Before a player receives and controls the ball he can make a feint to deceive his opponent and thus give himself more time and space.

4 v 4 line soccer

Modified rules:
- Goals can be scored by dribbling over the opposition's goal line.

Characteristics
Own side in possession:
- Goals are scored by dribbling over the opposition's goal line.
- Encourage 1 v 1 situations by means of positional play.

Opponents in possession:
- Defend well by means of positional play.
- Force opponent to play square.
- Regain the ball.

Demands of the game:
Own side in possession:
- Ball control in positional game.
- Act quickly, ability to pass directly.
- Overview in situations prior to switching the play, choosing the moment and the direction for beating an opponent, cutting across an opponent and shielding the ball.

Opponents in possession:
- Keep the ball in sight.

Dribbling is an important element in line soccer.

- Prevent opponents from scoring with out conceding a free-kick.
- Retain view of field, see more than the direct opponent (cover).

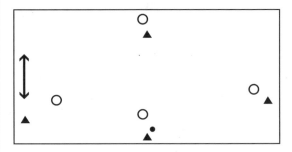

Dimensions, depending on age and level of skill:
>   length: 22 yards
>   width: 44 yards

Technical skills needed for this game:

Dribbling and running with the ball

When should a player dribble or run with the ball ?
- Moving slowly with the ball in a restricted space (dribbling).
- Running with the ball at greater speed when more space is available.

Focusing points for the technical execution
- Kicking leg
  Touch the ball so that it can be moved under control at running speed and in the correct direction (as if connected to an elastic band).
- Kicking foot
  Correct tension in foot and ankle (don't allow the ball to get too far ahead).
- Point of contact
  Propel the ball alternately with instep and inside and outside of foot, depending on change of direction.
- Body
  Upper body slightly over the ball; use arms   to maintain balance.

- Running
  Knees slightly bent (not a track athlete's stride).
- Pay attention to (observe):
  - surroundings (game situation)
  - the field close to the ball (uneven surface)

Passing with the inside of the foot

(see page 118)

Receiving and controlling the ball

(see page 118)

Sliding tackle

When should a sliding tackle be used?
- Last opportunity to:
  1. Prevent an opponent from shooting at goal, crossing the ball.
  2. Gain possession.
- Only make a sliding tackle if you are certain of reaching the ball and, preferably, winning it; otherwise stay on your feet!

Focusing points for the technical execution

Sliding at the ball when running at top speed:
- Supporting leg
  From close to, or diagonally behind, the opponent, bend leg strongly when taking final step.

- Body
  Body at full stretch.

- Kicking leg
  Pull kicking leg back (taut).

- Slide at the ball and, depending on the area of the pitch and the distance from the opponent, decide to
  - kick the ball away with the tip of the foot
  - pass the ball with the instep
  - gain possession by hooking the foot around the ball and then bending the knee while the body continues sliding.

Passing with the inside of the foot: the sequence of movements.

4 v 4
with 2 full-size goals

Characteristics
Own side in possession:
• Scoring goals.
• Run into space with or without the ball.
• Put teammates into scoring positions, deliver ball accurately.
• Restart by goalkeeper is important.
Opponents in possession:
• Prevent attempts to score.
• Goalkeeper's handling of shots at goal.

Demands of the game:
Own side in possession:
• Goal-oriented.
• Good positional game.
• When ball is free, shoot.
• Beat opponent in order to get into space with the ball.

• Goalkeeper must throw or roll the ball out accurately and at the right speed.

Opponents in possession:
• Mark the player in possession tightly.
• Don't allow yourself to be passed.
• Don't fall back towards your own goal.
• Block shots.
• Deal with shots on goal.

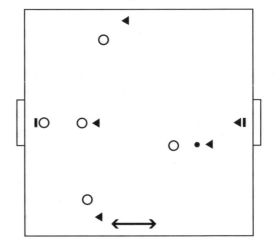

Dimensions, depending on age and level of skill:
　　length: 33 yards
　　width: 33 - 38 yards

In this game the players frequently have to kick the ball with the instep.

It must be possible to score from any-where on the field!

Technical skills needed for this game:

Kicking with the instep

When should a player kick the ball with the instep?
• When shooting at goal.

Focusing points for the technical execution
• Good position relative to the ball.
• <u>Supporting leg:</u>
With final large step, place supporting leg beside, just past, or behind the ball, with the tip of the foot pointing in the direction of play and the knee slightly bent.
  • Supporting leg slightly past the ball -> ball stays low
  • Supporting leg slightly behind the

ball, kicking foot under the ball -> ball flies up.
• <u>Body:</u>
  • Bent back (taut)
  • Leaning sideways over supporting leg (make space for shooting foot)
  • Bent forward at instant of shooting (explosive).
• <u>Kicking leg:</u>
  • From hip and knee, draw leg back, then swing it forward.
• <u>Kicking foot:</u>
  • Point toes down and lock ankle tight.
• <u>Point of contact</u>
  • Inside or full instep, depending on situation.

Passing with the inside of the foot
(see page 118)

Receiving and controlling the ball
(see page 118)

Players in the 10 to 12 age group can progress quickly if they are given good instruction. The technique shown in the first photo is far from perfect, but the second photo shows that a powerful shot has just been made. The two photos were taken 10 minutes after each other.

4 v 4
on a long, narrow pitch

Characteristics
Own team in possession:
- After winning the ball, hit a forward pass as quickly as possible.

Opponents in possession:
- Exert immediate pressure on opponents' buildup.

Demands of the game:
Own team in possession:
- Always be ready to play the ball forward.
- Ability to free the ball.
- Good positional play in restricted space as preparation for forward pass.
- Short 1-2 combinations and ball takeovers.
- Good cooperation (communication) between buildup players and forward player.

Opponents in possession:
- Defend towards the ball.
- Close off the line of play to the striker.

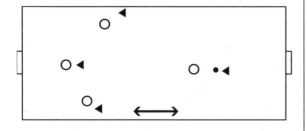

Dimensions, depending on age and level of skill:
length: 45 yards
width: 11 - 17 yards

Technical skills needed for this game:

Kicking with the instep

When should a player kick the ball with the instep?
- When shooting at goal.
- When hitting a long ball to switch play.

Focusing points for the technical execution
- Good position relative to the ball.
- Supporting leg:
  With final large step, place supporting leg beside, just past, or behind the ball, with the tip of the foot pointing in the direction of play and the knee slightly bent.
  - Supporting leg slightly past the ball -> ball stays low
  - Supporting leg slightly behind the ball, kicking foot under the ball -> ball flies up.
- Body
  - Bent back (taut), and bent forward at instant of shooting (explosive).
  - Leaning sideways over supporting leg (make space for the shooting foot)
- Kicking leg:
  - From hip and knee, draw leg back, then swing it forward.
- Kicking foot:
  - Point toes down, and lock ankle tight.
- Point of contact
  - Instep.

Passing with the inside of the foot

Why should a player use the inside of the foot?
- Accuracy
- Fast, short play (positional game).

Focusing points for the technical execution

4 v 4 with 2 small goals

(Emphasis on headed goals, suitable for older youngsters)

Modified rules:
Depending on the flow of the game, the coach can take the following measures:
- Goals can only be scored with headers and from outside the 18-yard line.
- Free zone at the sides of the pitch (5 yards wide).

Characteristics
Own side in possession:
- Score headed goals.
- Release players via the flanks.
- Long-range shots.
- Restart by goalkeeper is important.

Opponents in possession:
- Handling of high balls by goalkeeper.
- Defensive headers.
- Prevention of long-range shots.

Demands of the game:
Own team in possession:
- Good positional play to bring wingers into position.
- Specialists play in their specific positions.
- Intensive ball circulation.
- Good ball control: passing, receiving and controlling, beating an opponent, crossing, heading and shooting.
- Good restarts by goalkeeper: throw or roll the ball accurately and at the right speed.

Opponents in possession:
- Good positional defense.
- Defend close to the ball to prevent crosses and long-range shots.
- Good defensive technique: blocking tackles, sliding tackles, winning the ball (no fouls).
- Handling high balls (crosses): catching, punching, flicking over the bar.

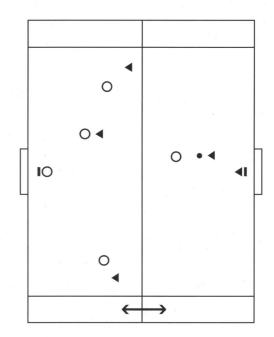

Dimensions, depending on age and level of skill:
length: 36 yards (= 2 x penalty area)
width: 45 - 50 yards

Technical skills needed for this game:

Heading

When should a player head the ball?
- High balls (both in defense and attack)

Focusing points for the technical execution

General:
Heading from a standing position
- Timing:
- Correct moment to meet the ball.
- Correct moment to jump for the ball.
- Arched body
  Just prior to meeting the ball, the body is arched backwards and the knees are bent.
- Legs:
  Movement initiated from the legs; stretch the knees.
- Body:

- From being arched backwards, arch powerfully forwards
- Meet the ball when the body is vertical.
- Head:
  Pull in the chin, keep the neck taut.
- Point of contact:
  Center of forehead.

Specifics:
Heading from a standing position, while turning. Header to the right, move right leg back.
- Upper body turns in direction of header.

Jump and head forward:
- Jump early after final long stride.
- Arch take-off leg backwards.
- Free leg bent and raised forward.
- Ball must be headed at the highest point of the jump.

Jump and head while turning:
- Header to the right, take off on right leg, start to turn.
- Free leg supports the jump (height) and the turn (direction).
- Shoulders turn explosively and the ball is met squarely from the arched position.

Kicking with the instep

When should a player kick the ball with the instep?
- When shooting at goal.
- When crossing.

Focusing points for the technical execution
(see page 123)

Crosses are a frequent feature of this game.

4 v 4 on a short, wide field (with one goalkeeper)

This game is especially suitable for coaching players to carry out tasks.

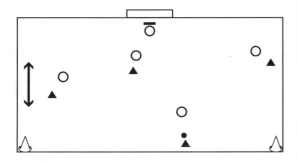

Dimensions:
Length: 22 yards
Width: 44 yards

Modified rules

- 1 full-size goal with a net and 1 goalkeeper.
- Other team defends the whole width of the pitch (44 yards).
- Team with goalkeeper can only score by dribbling the ball over the line.

Characteristics:

Possession: team A (O):

Good positional play, keeping the ball moving quickly, enables rapid switches across the width of the pitch, resulting in scoring opportunities.

When in possession they are confronted with more personal marking, which will result in more individual initiatives and short 1-2 combinations in order to be able to score in the goal (the security resulting from the fact that team A has a goalkeeper plays an important role).

Possession: team B (▼):

Team A must defend well positionally (whole line).

- Goalkeeper must read the game well and learn to recognize situations promptly and react appropriately.

Demands of the game when own team/opponents have possession

Own team in possession:

- Team A in possession:
  The ball must be kept moving at speed; 1-touch or 2-touch play.
- Team B in possession:
  The ball must be played carefully. The extreme pressure exerted by the opposition puts considerable demands on individual technical skills such as beating a man, dribbling, 1-2 combinations, insight and overview. Shoot at goal whenever an opportunity arises.

Concentrating on the anticipated cross.

Opponents in possession:

- **Team A in possession:**
  When team A is in possession the players of team B must mark their opponents closely and stay close to the ball. They can challenge for the ball because they have the safeguard of a goalkeeper. Considerable demands are made on technical ability in a defensive context (running at the right speed, feinting to challenge, challenging for the ball at the right moment, tackling with a view to winning the ball).

- **Team B in possession:**
  Team B must read the right moment to regain the ball. Caution is important, because being beaten is 'fatal'. Defend well positionally, be mobile, retain a good view of the situation around the ball and of direct opponent(s).

- Communication between the players of team B must be good when team A has the ball. Never lose sight of the situation, always keep the ball in view. In this way you can read what is expected of you and what solution is required.

- Besides defending his goal, the goalkeeper has an important role in the buildup, e.g. in switching quickly to buildup and attack when he has intercepted the ball.

Switch quickly after losing the ball; pressure the player in possession.

4 v 4 with 2 small goals and boards, specifically for the youngest players (6 - 10 years old)

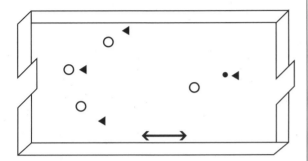

Dimensions:
Length: 44 yards
Width: 22 yards
- Small goals
- Boards, e.g. 1 yard high (or in a gymnasium, involving playing the ball off the walls).

Characteristics
- Because the ball (almost) never goes out, this game is eminently suitable for all age groups. In a very short time they are repeatedly confronted with new situations which require (technical)

solutions.
- The soccer obstacle "goal-orientedness" is helped by the boards. Even unsuccessful actions have no serious consequences, and the ball is soon worked towards the goals again.
- This game also demands creativity from the players, because they can play the ball off the walls as an extra aid (the wall is therefore a sort of extra teammate).
- Thanks to this aid the game is totally different to a game with lines. For older players the limited space created by the lines is an obstacle which can create a useful learning situation. Age and/or experience therefore play a role here.

Demands of the game
- Besides the usual positional play, this game provides other opportunities of playing via the boards (1-2 combinations).
- Defenders must take account of the "threat" of moves via the boards (it can be agreed beforehand whether play via the ends is permitted).
- The most important aspect of this game is that a lot of demands are made on players' technical skills and control of the ball in a very short time: dribbling, shielding the ball, passing, kicking, stopping the ball, feinting, shooting, etc.

The boards keep the ball in play.

4 v 4 with time running out (e.g. only 3 minutes to play)

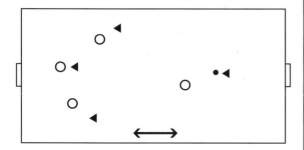

All variations of 4 v 4 can be used for this game.

Characteristics
- The team in possession must score (suggest a deficit).

- The team which is not in possession must regain the ball (e.g. they are one goal behind and can force overtime by scoring).

- The team in possession must not give the ball away or lose it (e.g. score is 1-0 and the aim is to play out time).

Also:
The scenarios referred to above must be introduced by the coach.
The coach must create a scenario in which certain behavior and activities are required from the players.

Demands of the game
- Depending on the scenario there are a number of important conditions.
  - Physical capabilities
    (Can you keep it up?).
  - Technical skills (Will the ball be won? Will the ball be held onto?).

- Mental aspects (concentration, communication, insight, perseverance).

- In situations where time is running out there is a tendency to force things. Players may defend too aggressively -> fouls. They may attack too hurriedly -> loss of possession. There may be a breakdown in communications -> mis-understandings -> loss of possession. Two defenders may go towards the player in possession -> inadequate communication.

- If the opposing team exerts pressure on the ball (they need it badly), this makes demands on skills such as shielding the ball, beating a man, selling a dummy, short 1-2 combinations, etc.).

- Making the best use of the available space when in possession is a key requirement.

. . .just 3 minutes to play, . . .and one goal behind!

4 v 4 with 3 teams

All variations of 4 v 4 can be used for this game.

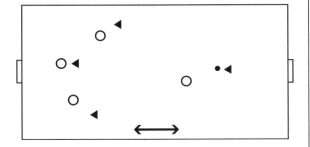

• When a goal is scored the scoring team remains on the pitch and the team that conceded the goal is replaced by the third team. Each team can remain on the pitch a maximum of 5 times.

• The team that is not playing can take a period of "relative rest" by playing a 3 v 1 positional game. Depending on the players' level of ability, features can be introduced such as allowing the ball to be touched just once, or a number of times, or the size of the playing area can be changed, or the rule for switching teams can be changed (e.g. when the ball is intercepted).

Therefore:

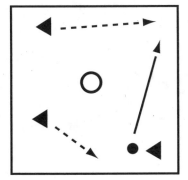

Important characteristics

• The tension involved in being able to stay on the pitch when a goal is scored and having to leave it when a goal is conceded creates a competitive atmosphere, which is in effect another soccer obstacle.

* If a team stays on the field several times in succession (i.e. wins frequently), this acts as a stimulus for the two weaker teams to force the stronger one out. It is important that, despite this strong motivation, the game is played in a controlled manner in accordance with the rules.

Demands of the game

• The rules agreed for the relevant 4 v 4 variation.

4 v 4 competition

This can be won by one individual player, and can be organized and supervised by 1 youth coach or manager.

Characteristics
- Each player plays each game with 3 "new" players.
- Each game is played on a different pitch.
- Each game is against a different opposing team.
- The players themselves monitor observance of the rules, keep score and inform the coach of the result.

- Self-motivation and initiative of the players are very important elements in this approach.

- Players are awarded points for a win, a draw, and goals scored.

Demands of the game
- Scoring lots of goals in a short time is a prerequisite for a good final classification.
- Good communication with the "new" players is essential before and during the games in order to reach agreement on distribution of tasks.
- The better the cooperation (communication), the higher the score and the more individual points are won.

A competition introduces suspense and rivalry.

CHAPTER 9
WHY 7 AGAINST 7?

Not too long ago, all soccer players, young and old, played 11 against 11. As soon as a youngster joined a club, he or she was "thrown in at the deep end". When the technical department of the Dutch Soccer Association began to look into how youngsters learn to play soccer, it soon became clear that 11 against 11 is not very suitable for young children.

The training and coaching objectives for each age category are described on page 28. Children are usually 5 to 8 years old when they start to play soccer, and at this age they mainly need to "master" the ball. "The ball should become your best friend." It is clear that many of the players in a game of 11 against 11 will experience only a few ball contacts, although frequent repetition (in this case frequent ball contacts) is the most important principle of learning. When some of these games were monitored, it was found that several children did not have a single ball contact!

The second reason for rejecting 11 against 11 for the youngest children is the size of the pitch. Not only does a game of 11 against 11 involve a large number of players, but the playing area is also much too large. The children cannot cope with all this space. The distances between the players are too great, and they are scarcely capable of bridging them.

Soccer is about scoring goals and preventing the opposition from scoring. If the players can barely reach the opposing team's goal, and there is therefore no continuous relationship between attacking and defending (it takes too long for the ball to reach the other end of the pitch), the events on the pitch bear little resemblance to a game of soccer. Moreover, the youngsters cannot learn anything from it.

The number of players (11 against 11) and the dimensions of the playing area (full-size pitch) allow far too many options and choices. Furthermore, too few players are involved in the game, and the objectives of the game are not achieved.

It was therefore decided that there should be "no games of 11 against 11 until age 11." In practice sense this means that youngsters below the age of 11 play their weekly competitive games in the 7 against 7 format.

How "7 against 7"
fits into the soccer learning process

Influence in the training areas depends on:
1. The age of the players.
2. The experience (soccer age) of the players.
3. The level of the players.
4. The available practice time.

Seniors and juniors:
11 against 11
(competitive games / practice games)
Before starting, define objectives, specify how to play, team formation, etc.

Games during training sessions
(11 against 11)
The coach is the referee; he can stop the game and intervene.

Small sided games during training sessions
(8 against 8 / 7 against 7)
The coach can stop the game and intervene.

Youngest children:
7 against 7 for the youngest children
(competitive games / practice games)
(Aims and basic principles of the main situations; global definition of tasks within the confines of the method of playing and the team formation)

From 8 year-olds to adults:
games and game related activities during training
(all the variations of 4 against 4 / small sided games between numerically unequal teams)
The coach teaches, stops the game and intervenes.

From second-year beginners to adults:
drills during training
basic drills:
- 1 against 1
- 4 against 4 and variations
- positional games
  (keep away, and going to goal)
- line soccer

The coach teaches, stops the game and intervenes.

First-year beginners (preliminary phase):
drills during training
drills for the preliminary phase

Is it possible to speak of fixed positions here?

Objectives for learning soccer tasks and functions

(Positions to take up when in possession and when possession has been lost)

Basic formation when in possession

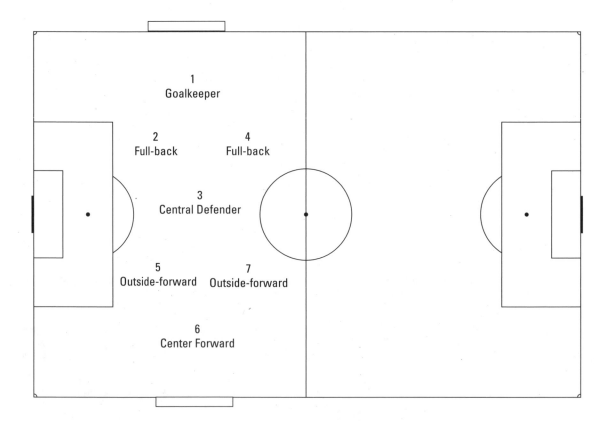

Tasks and functions associated with the different positions in 7 against 7

Tasks and functions per position:

Goalkeeper (1):
- Take up position in relation to the defenders
- Restart play by rolling, throwing, passing or kicking the ball
- Act as central build-up player (additional field player)

Full-backs (2 and 4):
- Take up position (well apart; make the playing area as wide as possible)
- Play the ball to the attackers
- If there is space, move forward with the ball
- Participate in the attack

Central defender (3):
- Take up position (between attackers and full-backs)
- Play the ball to the attackers or defenders who are participating in the attack
- If there is space, move forward with the ball
- Participate in the attack
- Try to score if the opportunity arises

Outside-forwards (5 and 7)
- Take up position in relation to the defenders (make the playing area as long as possible)
- Take the ball towards the opposition goal as quickly as possible (individual run) or pass to a teammate who has a clear run on goal

- Take up position in front of goal (available to receive a pass and score)
- Try to score

Center-forward (6):
- Get forward as far as possible (make the playing area as long as possible, while remaining available to receive a pass)
- Try to score (individual run, or exchange of passes with teammates)
- Go to goal!

Basic formation when the opposition is in possession:

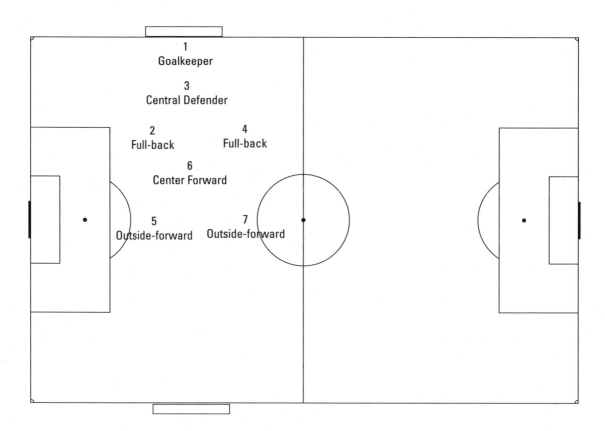

Tasks and functions per position:

Goalkeeper (1):
- Prevent the opposition from scoring
- Take up position in relation to the ball, the opposing players and teammates

Full-backs (2 and 4):
- DON'T LET YOURSELF GET BEATEN; prevent the opposition from scoring
- Cover the opposing attackers
- Help teammates (cover their backs)
- Win the ball

Central defender (3):
- DON'T LET YOURSELF GET BEATEN; prevent the opposition from scoring
- Cover the center-forward
- Help teammates (cover their backs)
- Make the playing area as small as possible
- Win the ball

Outside-forwards (5 and 7)
- Disrupt the opposition's build-up play
- Win the ball
- Help teammates (cover their backs)
- Make the playing area as small as possible
- DON'T LET YOURSELF BE PLAYED OUT

Center-forward (6):
- Cover the opposing central defender
- Disrupt the opposition's build-up play, prevent opponents from playing a long ball upfield
- Win the ball
- Help teammates (cover their backs)
- Make the playing area as small as possible
- DON'T LET YOURSELF BE PLAYED OUT

CHAPTER 10
GOALKEEPER TRAINING
by Frans Hoek

For a long time the goalkeeper did not receive the attention which he or she should get. This was mainly due to lack of understanding of the goalkeeper's very specialized position within the team. The widely held and frequently expressed opinion that "You have to be crazy to be a goalkeeper" certainly did not help the situation.

Fortunately, nowadays things are very different. A lot more is known about goalkeeping skills, and it is also recognized that good goalkeepers must possess a number of specific mental attributes.

The goalkeeper is part of the team. He is neither more nor less important than the other members of the team. Sometimes he will win a game for his team and sometimes he will lose one; on other occasions his performance will not affect the result one way or the other.

As part of the team the goalkeeper must receive the attention he needs to be able to function at his best. The goalkeeper's task is highly complex, and cannot be viewed in isolation from the task of the team as a whole.

Preventing goals, as many people describe the goalkeeper's task, is not easy.

Ideally the goalkeeper would work together so well with the rest of the team that the ball never comes near him.

If it does, the goalkeeper must handle it properly and try to increase his own team's chances of scoring. In practice this means that the goalkeeper must be the object of individual coaching in specific goalkeeping techniques and positional play, but he must also be integrated into the overall team training with all the real soccer obstacles, i.e. with teammates, opponents, etc.

Young goalkeepers

The coaching of goalkeepers is basically similar to the coaching of soccer players in general. Goalkeepers should participate normally in small sided and competitive games (e.g. 4 v 4). In view of the specific and special nature of goalkeeping skills (also for coaches), we restrict ourselves here to the most important elements of goalkeeping, as described in Frans Hoek's system of coaching for young goalkeepers.

The goalkeeper's main task: keeping the ball out of the net.

Philosophy of goalkeeping and goalkeeper training

The aim of the game

Before a team goes into a game, everyone who is involved must be aware of the ultimate objective. If this is not the case, this objective can never be achieved.

The goalkeeper, in common with his teammates, must make a positive contribution towards this objective, i.e. winning.

The goalkeeper's role in achieving this aim involves:

1. Making it as difficult as possible for the opposition to score.

2. Making the largest possible contribution to his own team's chance of scoring a goal.

If we look at the three main moments which arise during a game, and the associated objectives of the whole team, we can describe the specific task of the goalkeeper with some precision.

These three main moments are:

I.   Opponents in possession
II. Goalkeeper's team in possession
III. Change of possession from one team to the other

Opponents in possession
Aims of the whole team:
• disrupt opponents' buildup play;
• win the ball back;
• avoid conceding goals.

See Chapter 3 for the general starting points.

The goalkeeper's general tasks when the opposition is in possession
Depending on where the opposition has the ball, and on his strength and skills, the goalkeeper must take as active a role as possible by:
• communicating, organizing, taking command;
• positional play;
• intercepting the ball as early as possible.

Besides his general tasks, the goalkeeper also has specific tasks when the opposition is in possession.

Concentration. . .

A. During the game his specific tasks are:

1. <u>Communicating</u>
- ball at a safe distance from the goal;
- ball within shooting distance;
- ball between goalkeeper and defender.

2. <u>Positioning for:</u>
- long balls;
- lobs;
- 1 v 1 situations;
- crosses;
- shots and headers at goal.

3. <u>Dealing with the ball</u> (technique)
- adopting the "starting" posture;
- starting posture;
- footwork;
- jumping;
- catching;
- collapsing on the ball;
- diving;
- flicking;
- punching;
- airduels;
- 1 v 1 situation.

B. At restart situations his specific tasks are:

1. <u>Organizing his teammates at</u>
- drop ball;
- kick-off;
- throw-in;
- free-kicks;
- corners;
- penalties.

And also

2. <u>Communicating and giving instructions when</u>
- the ball is at safe distance from goal;
- the ball is within shooting distance.

3. <u>Positioning for</u>
- long balls;
- lobs;
- 1 v 1 situations;
- crosses;
- shots and headers at goal.

4. <u>Dealing with the ball</u> (technique)
- adopting the starting posture;
- starting posture;
- footwork;
- jumping;
- catching;
- collapsing;
- flicking;
- punching;
- airduels;
- 1 v 1 situation.

The goalkeeper's role when his team has possession??? Wouldn't it be better to play as sweeper?"

II. Goalkeeper's team in possession
Objectives of the whole team:

- retain possession;
- engage in buildup play to create chances;
- score goals.

See Chapter 5 for the general starting points.

The goalkeeper's general task when his team is in possession

Depending on what his teammates do, the goalkeeper's task is to facilitate good buildup play from which goals can be scored.

He must be able to distribute the ball to his front players, and he must not try to pass to teammates who are covered and therefore have little or no chance of gaining or holding the ball, especially in the vicinity of his goal, where no risks should be taken in buildup play.

The tasks of the goalkeeper are therefore:

- aim to play the ball as far forward as possible;
- retain possession;
- take no risks in buildup play near own goal.

Besides his general tasks, the goalkeeper also has specific tasks when his team is in possession

1. <u>The goalkeeper has the ball:</u>
Restart situations

A. Techniques for restart situations:
- drop-kick;
- volley;
- underarm throw;
- overhand throw;
- playing the ball with the feet (necessary after a backpass, or if the goalkeeper

catches the ball and decides to roll it forward before kicking it into play);
- goal-kick;
- free-kick.

B. The moment when the game is restarted (make a choice).

Instructing through:
- communication (in word and gesture) with the player receiving the ball;
- closing up/linking up of players when play is restarted.

2. <u>Teammates in the defensive line have the ball:</u>
The position of the goalkeeper must be such that:
- he is available to receive the ball;
- he can react adequately to the new situation if possession is lost.

Communication with:
- player in possession of the ball;

Goal-kicks should always go to a teammate.

- players around the ball.

3. <u>Teammates in midfield or attacking line have the ball:</u>

The position of the goalkeeper must be such that he can immediately react adequately to the new situation if possession is lost.

Communication with:
- defensive line;
- possibly the midfield line.

III. Transition: when there is a change in possession

<u>The objective is:</u>
- to switch quickly from the one objective to the other. The emphasis is on speed!

Change of possession

See Chapter 3 for the general starting points.

The goalkeeper must always be prepared to join in actively at these crucial moments (communicating, intercepting the ball as early as possible, playing a role in restart situations).

The goalkeeper's general task:

1. <u>Quickly switch from the one objective to the other in terms of:</u>
- posture;
- communicating.

Goalkeeper coaching

The goalkeeper may have to cope with a number of obstacles and complicating factors such as:
- the ball;
- opponents;
- teammates;
- laws of the game;
- goal-orientedness;
- stress;
- time;
- space;
- material.

A goalkeeper must develop technique, insight and communicative skills, always taking account of the above factors. These components - technique, insight and communication - can be distinguished from each other, but always belong together.

The 1 v 1 situation

1 v 1 situations are very important for a goalkeeper. When a single attacker confronts the goalkeeper the pressure is almost always on the attacker. He must score from this excellent chance. The goalkeeper is the innocent victim, much as when he faces a penalty. If he is beaten everyone simply shrugs, but if he saves the ball he is a hero. Looked at in this way, the goalkeeper is always the underdog in such situations.

However, this is a false perception. In fact, a goalkeeper has a 70% chance of winning such a confrontation. This means that he should win 7 out of 10 such duels.

In this case winning does not just mean parrying or catching the ball. It also counts as a success if the attacker shoots wide or over the bar, or is forced so wide that there is no longer any immediate danger, or is delayed so long that a defender can take the ball from him.

How a goalkeeper can increase his chance of winning a 1 v 1 confrontation is described below.

Choose the right moment to intervene!

Problems from the point of view of the goalkeeper

I. The goalkeeper's position

This must be such that:

- The goal is always defended;
- there is a maximum chance of intercepting the ball or delaying the attacker.

The exact position which the goalkeeper will adopt depends on a number of factors, such as:

1. The goalkeeper's attributes;
2. Factors relating to the player facing the goalkeeper, such as:
- speed of approach;
- technical ability;
- line of approach.
3. Position of teammates and whether one or more of them can reach the ball.

An old head on young shoulders!

4. Weather conditions, state of the pitch.

Concrete guidelines and tips:

The goalkeeper's position will in principle change continuously if an opponent breaks through alone from the center line. In general:

In a 1 v 1 confrontation

1. Always stand on the imaginary line joining the ball and the center of the goal.
2. Always stand in front of the goal line:
- position yourself at a distance from the goalline that:
   a. ensures you can get back to intercept a lob if necessary, or;
   b. gets you so close to the attacker that he cannot lob you.

This is a very important aspect of 1 v 1 duels!

As the goalkeeper changes his position it is important that, when the attacker touches the ball, the goalkeeper adopts or has adopted the starting posture, so that he can react to the new situation.

II. Starting posture, options, dealing with the ball, and the subsequent action

When the goalkeeper has taken up his ideal position, the attacker's position and options play an important role. This is made clearer by the following descriptions of various situations.

First of all, however, a few words about the goalkeeper's starting posture, which plays an important role in 1 v 1 confrontations:

Starting posture no. 1
The posture for dealing with shots at goal.

Starting posture no. 2
The posture for getting close to an

attacker to increase the chance of intercepting lobs and shots.

Starting posture no. 3
The posture for reacting to either a long
ball or a lob.

*Situation: A single opponent bears down on
the goalkeeper from the center line. How
must the goalkeeper react?*

The following scenarios may arise:

1. The goalkeeper stands in his ideal
   position in the correct posture (starting
   posture no. 3) and assesses whether the
   attacker has pushed the ball far enough
   ahead to be intercepted. If this is the
   case, the goalkeeper goes out to deal
   with the ball.

He deals with the ball
   - by reaching it before the attacker can
     touch it again;
   - by reaching it at the same moment as
     the attacker (block tackle);
   - by reaching it after the attacker
     touches it again (usually this means
     that the goalkeeper is too late).

If possible, the goalkeeper should
ensure that his team retains possession
of the ball. However, his first priority is
to avoid taking any risks, in view of the
fact that the goal is totally undefended
and loss of possession could therefore
result in a goal. If danger threatens he
should kick the ball upfield or over the
sideline.

The goalkeeper must then get back into
position in the penalty area in order to
be able to react to the new situation.

2. The attacker maintains sufficiently close
   control of the ball to exclude an
   interception. The goalkeeper must then:

   - run back (proper footwork) to a new
     position, because the player with the
     ball is getting closer;
   - be standing still in the correct starting
     posture when the attacker touches the
     ball again;
   - assess whether or not he can intercept
     the ball after the attacker touches it
     again.

3. The attacker keeps close control of the
   ball and the goalkeeper has to go back.
   A goalkeeper should, in principle, never
   retreat beyond the edge of the goal
   area. From here, the goalkeeper must
   confront the attacker. How?
   - he must always be mentally and
     physically alert in order to be able to
     take full advantage of the opportunity
     if the attacker pushes the ball a little
     too far ahead, by:
   a. intercepting the ball before the
      attacker can touch it again;
   b. throwing himself at the attacker's
      feet at the moment when he
      touches the ball again, or just
      afterwards;
   c. getting as close as possible to the
      attacker to give himself the best
      possible chance of reaching a shot
      or a lob, provided his position and
      starting posture are correct.

In this way:
- the attacker is slowed down, giving
  the goalkeeper and possibly the
  defenders a better chance;
- the attacker is forced to go wide in
  order to take the ball round the
  goalkeeper, giving the goalkeeper and
  possibly the defenders a better
  chance;
- if the attacker shoots, there is a greater
  chance that he will hit the goalkeeper
  or, in trying to avoid the goalkeeper,
  will shoot wide.

If the goalkeeper wins possession of the ball, he needs to have a fast transition and start the buildup. If the ball is only deflected the goalkeeper needs to focus on the new situation which has developed.

Important points:

Patience
- It is the attacker who is under pressure. In 9 cases out of 10 he will make a mistake by pushing the ball too far forward under pressure from one or more opponents, or because of the poor state of the pitch, or because his technique is not good enough. The goalkeeper must be alert for these moments, so that he can exploit them properly.
- Many goalkeepers "sell" themselves too quickly by going down feet-first, etc. This plays into the attacker's hands. He can lob the ball over the goalkeeper, or go round him with a simple movement. A goalkeeper should only go down if he is 99.999% sure that he will at least touch the ball.
  Going down too early is not a good move, because the goalkeeper then needs too long to recover if he does not get the ball.
- The goalkeeper must be thoroughly familiar with the laws of the game and the serious consequences of any offense he may commit in a 1 v 1 situation. Handling the ball outside the penalty area is punished with a red card, as is bringing down a player who has broken through outside the penalty area.
- Working together with teammates is absolutely crucial.
  As soon as there is a chance that a teammate can get to the ball, the goalkeeper must in principle decide not to go out towards the attacker or the ball.

Giving instructions to teammates
- The goalkeeper must tell his teammates whether they should challenge for the ball or cover his back.
  Cooperation is very important. Prior agreements must be reached, the calls to be used must be discussed, and everyone must practice using them.

Choices
It is clear that the goalkeeper must constantly make choices: "Should I stay back or go out?", "Can a defender get back to make a challenge?", etc. Practice these situations, and once a decision is made, stick to it, even if appears to be wrong.

In the beginning it is important to learn from mistakes. A goalkeeper can build on this experience to cut down on the number of errors.

The backpass

At the start of the 1992-93 season, a rule was introduced concerning passes back to the goalkeeper. The goalkeeper was no longer allowed to pick up a backpass but had to play it with his feet. This rule caused a lot of fuss. In particular, goalkeepers with underdeveloped ball-playing skills were far from enthusiastic. However, for goalkeepers with good soccer technique, the change had the effect of making the game more interesting.

Reactions to the rule were varied. In England almost all backpasses were simply booted upfield. In the Netherlands a more tactical approach is favored, and it is the task of the goalkeeper to help his team retain possession and to initiate a new attacking buildup.

The main problem with the rule is the definition of what is and is not a backpass. When can the goalkeeper handle the ball and when not?

The rule forces the goalkeeper to take a

different approach, to be aware of the new situation and to implement the best solution as quickly as possible.

Many goalkeepers were able to make the necessary adjustments within a short time. The backpass rule has improved the game. In particular, the goalkeeper's game has been given a new and important dimension. The goalkeeper's ability to influence the outcome of a game in a positive or negative sense has been increased.

Because many goalkeepers still experience considerable problems with the backpass, we will deal with this subject in detail.

Problems from the goalkeeper's point of view

I. <u>The position of the goalkeeper</u>
The position must be such that:
- the goal always is or can be defended;
- the goalkeeper is available to receive a backpass;
- the distance between the player who makes the backpass and the goalkeeper is as large as possible (= more time and space).

II. <u>If the player makes a backpass</u>
Assess the overall situation:
- pace of the ball;
- positions of teammates and opponents;
- depending on the above, make a choice: play the ball first time; bring it under control and play it; bring it under control;
- dribble the ball or play it.

Important points:

- early instructions from goalkeeper;
- never take any risks (it is better to concede a corner than a goal);
- 'ideally' the ball should be kept within the team and, depending on the

Goalkeeper coach Frans Hoek explains how to choose the right position.

situation, played to:
- a forward;
- a midfielder;
- a defender.

If this is impossible, hit a long ball upfield:
- out-of-play, as far away from the goal as possible;
- possibly give away a corner.
- If an opponent challenges, do not try to beat him for the sake of beating him (in the same way as, for example, an attacker), but only to make sufficient space to be able to pass the ball properly.
- Try to pass to the goalkeeper's strongest foot (in cooperation with teammates).
- Practice kicking with both feet, because sometimes you have to use your weaker foot.
- Get your teammate to play the ball as soon as possible, so that you have more time and space. The teammate must then run into space as fast as possible

(perhaps after first 'blocking' an opponent) to make himself available for a pass.

Penalty kick competition; what can the goalkeeper win?

Development of ball-playing skills by the goalkeeper

The goalkeeper must develop the ball-playing skills that he needs to deal with backpass situations.

What skills does he need?

The goalkeeper must learn to approach a backpass in the same way as an outfield player.

When a goalkeeper has the ball in his hands it is safe; no one can take it from him. But a backpass is fair game for everyone. The goalkeeper must be able to play the ball directly; or bring it under control and play it; or bring it under control, dribble it and play it.

He must be able to do this with either foot. The overall situation determines where the ball should be played to. A good overview of the field is very important in this context.

Exercises in which these skills can be practiced include:
- positional games (3 v 1, 4 v 2 or 5 v 2);
- small sided games;
- specific exercises such as passing, kicking.

The problem of the goal, and the last man in front of the goal must always be taken into account. This means that you must first ensure that the backpass cannot cross the goal line, and then that the ball can be brought back into play.

Important points, especially for the goalkeeper (but also for the other players) are:

The ball must be passed back in such a way that it cannot cross the line if the goalkeeper misses it, i.e. minimize the risk of an own-goal.

This means that a player who passes back must weight the pass properly, must direct it at the goalkeeper's strongest foot, and must make the pass as early as possible (to give the goalkeeper more time and space). After passing the ball to the goalkeeper, the player must take up a position so that he can receive the ball again if needed.

For the goalkeeper this means:

- take no risks, as wide and as far forward as possible;

- decide quickly: play the ball first time or bring under control first (partly depends on limitations: 1-touch play, 2-touch play, play the ball into space).

Read the play, and take up the right position.

The long ball

One of the situations for which goal-keepers are least prepared is dealing with a long ball forward or a through pass in and around the penalty area. There are many reasons for this state of affairs, but in principle it is unacceptable, because this is an essential aspect of goalkeeping in the modern game.

If a team plays most of its soccer in its opponents' half (like Ajax Amsterdam), it is clear that there will be a lot of space between its defenders and its goal line. The responsibility for defending this space obviously belongs with the goalkeeper.

This is logical. But as soon as the space behind the defenders narrows (e.g. between the edge of the penalty area and the goal line), the goalkeeper's role is much less logical and clear cut in the eyes of many coaches. Nevertheless, the goal-keeper must always try to control and defend the space in front of his goal.

Intercepting

Stanley Menzo is rarely surprised by a lob.

The goalkeeper must intercept the ball as soon as possible. This is an important basic principle of the philosophy of goalkeeping and goalkeeper training when the opposition is in possession.

This can be achieved by controlling the final part of the pitch. Many factors are involved in dealing with a long ball, so the situation is very complex.

In general, however, there is little appreciation of the mastery of this impor-tant aspect. If a goalkeeper comes out and intercepts a long ball, most people tend to think that this was easy and the opponent simply made a bad pass. However, if a goalkeeper fails to deal with a through ball and a goal then results, he is criticized because it is clear that it was his fault. This is not fair.

Consider the following situation. If a goalkeeper always remains on his line, he runs no risk of making a recognizable mistake.

Nevertheless such a tactic results in more scoring opportunities for the opposition, although this is less apparent. Such a goalkeeper will also be confronted with more 1 v 1 situations, and what chance does he have then?

It is therefore better to try to intercept long balls. It is preferable to make 50 good interceptions and one blunder during the course of a season than to be confronted 51 times with a 1 v 1 situation! That is the real choice he faces. It has been stated above that a good goalkeeper has a 70% chance of winning a 1 v 1 duel. But in the case under consideration this would mean conceding 19 goals! Naturally it is important that the goalkeeper trains and practices for this situation. First of all, therefore, this soccer problem must be analyzed point by point.

Problems from the goalkeeper's point of view

The general lack of appreciation, and

fear of the consequences of making a mistake, cause many goalkeepers to be afraid of missing a long ball or a lob.

Goalkeepers therefore prefer to remain on the line, and this results in more 1 v 1 situations. A goalkeeper feels that in a 1 v 1 duel he will be a hero if he prevents a goal by making a fantastic save, but even if a goal is scored he will not be blamed, because everyone can appreciate how difficult such a situation is. The coach's first task is to point out the flaw in this argument, although this will mean a whole new approach for most goalkeepers.

I. Position of the goalkeeper
This position must be such that:
- the goal is always defended;
- the goalkeeper controls as large an area as possible in front of goal.

These two requirements are closely connected. The more the goalkeeper stays on his line, the smaller is the area that he can control. The compensating factor is that he is unlikely to be beaten by a lob. The goalkeeper must stand as far off his line as possible while still being capable of dealing with a lob. This means that he must train very hard in dealing with this situation in order to dispel his fear of being lobbed.

This position also depends on a number of other factors. These factors are:
1. the goalkeeper's individual attributes;
2. considerations related to the player on the ball:
   - his position;
   - whether he is right- or left-footed;
   - his strength;
   - whether he is moving at speed or not.
3. weather conditions, state of the pitch;
4. position of teammates;
5. position of opponents;
6. type of ball.

This goalkeeper was caught napping

II. The starting posture
When the ball is well away from the goal, and the only danger is from a lob, the starting posture is the "stride" stance (feet apart, one foot forward, one foot back), because this allows the goalkeeper to set off fastest (forwards or backwards) to intercept either a long ball or a lob.

If the ball is closer to the goal, so that a shot is possible, the starting posture for dealing with shots should be adopted.

III. When the opponent hits the ball
1. Lob over goalkeeper
The lob will have to be dealt with safely.

Attention must be given to:
- starting posture;
- assessing the path of the ball;
- turning;
- footwork;
- push-off;
- handling the ball;
- follow-up action - rebound;
- corner
- buildup play.

2. <u>Long ball</u>
Attention must be given to:
a. assessing
   - the path of the ball;
   - teammates' chances of intercepting the ball;
   - opponents' options.

Focus training on how to deal with a lob.

b. making a decision and communicating this as early as possible to everyone who is affected.

The decision can be "go out" or "stay". Goalkeeper decides to stay

- The goalkeeper must make clear to his teammates that they should challenge for the ball if they can (communication). The goalkeeper must take up a new position, because the position of the ball has changed and he has to adjust to the new situation.

- It may be that neither the goalkeeper nor one of his teammates can get to the ball to intercept it. The goalkeeper must then take up a new position because the position of the ball has changed and he has to be ready for the new situation (e.g. 1 v 1, or a ball to the flank).

Goalkeeper decides to go out
   The goalkeeper must make it clear that he is going for the ball. This choice depends on the positions of his teammates. Reach prior agreement on the calls to be used, e.g. "leave it" or "mine".
   Any teammates in the goalkeeper's vicinity must let him go for the ball and must take up new positions (e.g. cover him). The goalkeeper must then take action to defuse the situation.

Attention must be given to:

- starting posture;
- footwork;
- dealing with the ball, and subsequently distributing it;
- follow-up action - rebound (or new position to deal with new situation);
   - buildup play.

Important: never take risks!
(except to prevent last-minute 0-1 in crucial match, etc.)

1. Laws of the game:
   • handling the ball - red card!
   • foul on opponent - red card!

2. Dealing with the ball (if possible):
   a. give it to a teammate (upfield);
   b. upfield = send it as far away as possible;
   c. send it over the sideline;
   d. concede a corner.

Quickly return to correct position, i.e. the position that gives you the best chance of defending your goal, and controlling a large area in front of it.

Why? As a goalkeeper you have to leave your position to deal with the ball. You are not allowed to use your hands, so you have to play it in the same way as a field player, and the ball remains playable by all players.

You are completely out of position, and the goal is in principle undefended if an opponent gets the ball or one of your teammates loses the ball (or the ball goes out of play and a quick throw-in is taken). The opposition therefore has a good chance to score.

The goalkeeper must assess whether the defender can intercept the long ball.

CHAPTER 11
CONDITIONING IS SOCCER TRAINING, SOCCER TRAINING IS CONDITIONING

A coach wants to influence and therefore improve the soccer playing ability of his charges. Knowledge of, and insight into, this ability is necessary in order to be able to analyze it. A knowledge of the specific obstacles (and difficulty factors) associated with soccer, and how to work with them, is the basis of soccer coaching.

When we think of physical training, also referred to below as conditioning, we usually think of tired and sore muscles, running, being hot, sweating, sprinting, carrying out power exercises. In short, all sorts of activities aimed at pushing the physical limitations of a player's performance. The principle is that the body adjusts to the increasing demands made on it.

The body must therefore always be asked to do slightly more than it is used to. However, a player's performance is more than the sum of his stamina, strength, speed, suppleness, technical skills, tactical insight, mental attitude, etc.

These factors have nothing to say about players' soccer ability. The important thing is how players solve the problems they encounter and achieve the objectives they set themselves during a game of soccer. An analysis must therefore be made of players' soccer ability. Obviously this will involve more than simply measuring muscle circumference, lung capacity, heartbeat, oxygen uptake, jumping power, etc. Nor do a player's figures for the 100 meter sprint and the Cooper twelve-minute test reveal anything about his ability to play soccer. Such an analysis is more concerned with the efficiency with which a player solves a soccer problem.

A definition of a player's conditioning in the context of soccer is: the degree to which the player is capable of making a positive contribution to the result of the game.

> The better the TIC (technique, insight, and communication), the better the player's conditioning.

The philosophy of the Dutch Soccer Association and conditioning/training

Conditioning often used to be focused on the muscles. The muscles, however, are the slaves of the brain. Muscles are incapable of learning. The brain learns. In order to learn to play soccer and to gain in proficiency, soccer must not be simplified in terms of movements but, in terms of the purpose of moving: the attainment of soccer objectives.

If a player knows the purpose of solving soccer problems, his brain will guide his muscles. The greater the player's experience in a given situation, the faster he will be able reach decisions.

Conditioning in soccer

Any consideration of conditioning in a soccer context must include the following aspects:

1. The degree to which a player is capable of making a positive contribution to the result of the game.

2. There must be a relationship with the specific obstacles encountered in the game of soccer.

3. The purpose is to attain soccer objectives.

4. An analysis of the degree to which players are capable of attaining the objectives within the context of the three main moments in a game of soccer.

5. Evaluate players by "Reading" the behavior of the players during the game. Therefore no pseudo-evaluations by way of, for example: Cooper test or shuttle test (is measuring .... knowing?).

6. Description of behavior:
   • quality: goal-orientedness, efficiency;
   • quantity: sufficiently long, continuous, frequent.

Physical training should be: systematically improving the quality of soccer play.

An evaluation of a game always contains remarks on performance.
For example: both when in possession, and when the opposition is in possession

• Ability to solve problems in a faster sequence.
• Continuously, in sequence.
• Under pressure from an opponent.
• Under pressure from spectators.
• Forcing with respect to opponent.
• Variation and the unexpected.
• Anticipation.
• Adjusting swiftly from possession to non-possession and vice versa.

> Playing, coaching and training have more to do with the head than the legs.

Application of theory

A coach must have a knowledge of the principles which apply to the development of stamina, strength, etc. These are the general principles of conditioning theory. Soccer ability is developed with the help of these principles, by applying them in practice (in small-sided games, competitive games, etc.).

This duel of strength is different to the strength required in a weightroom.

Besides a knowledge of conditioning theory, it is important to know how players learn, and how to teach soccer. There are no recipes for this, with ready-made solutions. In practice, a coach must apply his knowledge to his own situation. In the world of soccer this is difficult, because knowledge and insight are indispensable prerequisites for discussing the condition of soccer players.

It cannot be said that soccer players would play better if they had a larger lung capacity (this can easily be acquired by means of endurance exercises). Nor can it be said that players would play better or head the ball better if they had stronger leg muscles (also easily acquired in a gymnasium by performing leg extension exercises against resistance). Similarly it cannot be assumed that players would be better if they could run faster (something that is in any case difficult to train for).

Reading the game

The ability to read the game, i.e. recognize what is happening, is the most important attribute of a coach (see Chapter 5). In choosing the correct drill, method, mode of working and organization associated with a soccer situation, the most important aspect is to be able to describe the problem and to explain the correct diagnosis.

It should by now be clear that this diagnosis cannot be phrased in terms such as "He has to jump higher/ run faster/ make a more supple body-swerve, etc.". The problem must be formulated in clearly understandable soccer terms, capable above all of being understood by the players. They must be able to grasp what is lacking.

Soccer conditioning in practice

In practice, therefore, condition has everything to do with soccer. The coach must constantly try to create situations which will stimulate players to perform certain soccer actions better, more frequently in sequence, or faster. The principle of improving players' performances is based on doing things whose degree of difficulty steadily increases.

Soccer players are more motivated to sprint for a ball than to sprint for its own sake.

It is therefore essential that the circumstances under which a player performs (playing, competing, training) must demand just a little more of him than he is capable of. There must be a challenge which the player wants to accept (this is an absolute prerequisite) but which also arouse some apprehension. The player must be confronted by a difficult task, which requires concentration and a certain frame of mind. In the language of conditioning theory this is referred to as the overload principle.

Having to do more than you really can. This makes condition training more like a competitive game. However, in practice, (competitive games and training sessions) it is all too frequently the case that insufficient or no attention is paid to this principle.

If the greater part of soccer training does not conform to these principles, then it cannot really be called training (= improving performance), but simply keeps the status quo (which can be useful), provides something to do (less useful), or is boring (which is totally undesirable).

It must therefore be possible to make a given task more difficult (in competitive games but also and above all in training sessions), so that with a little good will (concentration), it can just be achieved. The coach must continuously monitor the situation in order to ensure that his charges keep trying to achieve soccer objectives.

In practice, the coach uses competitive and non-competitive games to improve his players' soccer ability. He doesn't simply set these games in motion, but coaches the players on the skills they have to develop in this situation.

The coach can do this in a number of ways. He can confront the players with situations in which they are forced to play in a specific manner.

Examples:

- Assigning a specific role or task, such as playing 1-on-1 at the back, or letting the striker act as a target man up front.
- Manipulating the number of opponents.
- Manipulating time and space parameters (size and shape of playing area).
- Manipulating the rules (offside, no offside, etc.).

The soccer situation must be solved in such a way that the players just succeed in performing the required soccer task. By organizing things so that players are forced to play in a certain way, a coach can influence aspects such as speed of action, choosing the correct solution, correct timing, etc.

Naturally the emphasis differs according to the age of the players. Other important factors are their level of skill, the objective to be achieved, and the time available for practice, and coaching.

Goalkeepers improve their goalkeeping ability by applying the same principles as field players.

In the context of improving soccer ability (condition), the phases of a soccer player's development are listed again here.

A. Preliminary phase (5-7 years)

- The basic techniques must be acquired during this phase.

  Typical remarks:
  "You must be able to kick, dribble, stop the ball, etc. in order to be able to take part in a game of soccer".
  "Ball control".

B. Phase 1 (7-12 years) Basic proficiency

- Learning how to solve soccer problems, with the emphasis on adapting to the situation.

  Typical remark:
  "You must be able to overcome the obstacles presented by your opponent, limited space, teammates in your vicinity, etc., and deal with the ball properly, choose the next move correctly, stop the ball dead, keep possession, pass it accurately, etc.".
  "Controlling the ball in typical soccer situations".

C. Phase 2 (12-16 years) Competitive proficiency

- Learning to solve soccer problems, with the emphasis on how choosing the correct option in respect of the player's position in the team or in a particular unit of the team (defensive line, etc.).

  Typical remark:
  "You must be able to combine with your teammates in order to get past an opponent. The most important thing is the result of what you do".

The ability to deal with an opponent's resistance.

D. Phase 3 (16-18 years) Competition proficiency

- Learning to win, and to use all available resources to achieve a good result. Thinking about and consciously working on the planned and systematic improvement of performance. The organization and intensity of training sessions becomes important. Use scrimmages to learn to face the systems, and opponents who you play against in competitive games.

  Typical remark:
  "Don't just think about yourself in isolation; play to achieve a result, carry out your own task within the team, communicate with your teammates, and keep an eye on the score and the remaining time."
  Own team in possession: "Retain possession, but be aggressive".
  Opposition in possession: "Defend actively, try to win the ball back".

Conditioning in practice: the youngest players

Objectives such as improving soccer ability in connection with obtaining better results in real competitive matches are of little interest in the context of the youngest players.

Very young players are more concerned with their own actions than with the result of their team or the functioning of its different units or its position in the league table. The condition (or referred to as soccer ability in our concept) of a very young player is more readily expressed in the way in which he deals with one of the first difficulty factors or obstacles in his soccer development, i.e. the ball.

This is one of the first requirements in the development of a child's soccer ability.

We have already indicated that learning to play soccer goes hand in hand with attempting to achieve soccer objectives, i.e. the important thing is:

dribbling in order to ...

passing in order to ...

shooting in order to ...

running in order to ...

jumping in order to ...

In the development phase in which players have just overcome the first difficulty factor, i.e. the ball, it is essential to "condition" them still further, i.e. to teach them how to handle other typical soccer obstacles such as:

- teammates;
- opponents;
- time/space;
- goal-orientedness;
- rules of the game;
- stress.

Learning how to deal with these factors is crucial for very young players. The process of learning how to deal with the ball (technical skills) in soccer-specific situations (in small sized and competitive games) will be constantly emphasized and developed. In short, the pupils must be encouraged to develop an insight into finding the correct solutions to the problems faced in a variety of soccer situations.

A few comments on earlier ideas on conditioning, especially in the context of young players, are perhaps appropriate here. It is of course to be welcomed when children are confronted with all sorts of movement exercises and physical exercises, e.g. during physical education at school. At the age when they are especially susceptible to such stimuli (influences) they should be presented with as varied a program as possible. This is also true of soccer training. Players aged 8-14 years can rapidly absorb and retain soccer experience, and recall it in similar situations.

The basic premise of this concept is that players should be confronted with soccer situations as frequently as possible during this phase of their development. Given the limited time available, it is pointless to force players to perform all sorts of exercises intended to develop more strength, a stronger heart, more stamina, etc., especially in view of the low enjoyment factor associated with such a regime.

If we watch games in this age group it is obvious that they do not suffer from the player's lack of stamina and strength, but rather from their lack of insight. Lack of mutual understanding and support is a problem of a far higher order than lack of strength. The development of a functional technical ability, directed towards what can be achieved in a given soccer situation, is central to the training of players.

Conditioning in practice: the older youth players

In the case of older players, the emphasis is on improving soccer ability in order to achieve a better result in competitive matches. The players must learn how to deal most effectively with the various opportunities, strong points, shortcomings, etc. within a team.

Important aspects include deciding on the best position for each player in the team (harnessing the skills of players to specific positions and functions), deciding what system to play, what formations to adopt when in possession and trying to regain possession, etc.

As has already been pointed out, a coach must read the match, describe problems, formulate objectives and create the best conditions (training/coaching situations) in line with the above mentioned principles; furthermore the basis of coaching must be the attempt to achieve playing objectives within the confines of the rules of the game. For example, a small sided game in which attackers play against defenders can be played (e.g. 5 v 4). The defenders (with one man less than the attackers) can be given the task of defending as actively as possible and attempting to win the ball.

If the defenders give away too many free kicks in carrying out this task, this negates the objective of the exercise, i.e. defending then switching from defense to buildup and attack. The coach will therefore have to intervene by giving instructions or explaining how the defenders can carry out their task better and more effectively, in line with their objectives. He can comment on tackling technique, positional play when the ball has been won, etc. If we examine this game in terms of conditioning, we can see that the emphasis is on giving content to this difficult task. The 4 defenders must work hard to regain the ball.

As players get older their horizon extends beyond the ball.

This puts considerable demands on players. The elements that drive and motivate the players are anchored in their task (i.e. to try to win the ball without being beaten). The players efforts to carry out this task set a variety of processes in motion in their bodies: heart, lungs, blood circulation, muscles, joints, metabolism, etc.

They are therefore not given a task such as: run faster, run longer, run more explosively so that your heart, lungs, blood circulation, muscle power, suppleness and coordination will be improved. But the body listens to what its master wants, i.e. to win the ball back, and obeys slavishly.

Naturally it can only do this up to a certain level. This is where the coach's expertise comes in. He has learned (or must know) that when players can no longer carry out their task - not because they make mistakes but because they are exhausted - then the limit has been reached. The players are too tired to mark tightly, to chase after the ball, to tackle properly.

In order to improve the players' performance in this area (keeping going for longer, winning the ball back faster, choosing the best option for the next move, etc.) they must be encouraged to keep going just a little longer, with suitable coaching, so that they can carry out their task reasonably successfully even under extremely difficult circumstances.

The coach's evaluation criteria are not heart rate, distance covered, number of pounds or time, but whether the players can still achieve the objective of the soccer task. He looks at the quality of what is offered, the yield, the time that the players hold out, the other tasks that can be carried out besides the specific task (overview), the willingness to keep trying or the tendency to give up (player becomes "invisible"), the ability to keep influencing teammates (communication).

Insight and understanding are important elements of soccer conditioning.

These criteria are closely related to the objective of the training activities. A coach who is skilled in playing with, or manipulating obstacles can illustrate, explain and emphasize certain objectives, and make them harder or easier. He is then, by definition, engaged in conditioning. To repeat: muscles cannot learn; the important thing is for objectives to be recognized. The body will then follow. Conditioning is not something that should be thought of in terms of physical factors. It is concerned with the inseparable connection between intellectual, emotional and physical elements. Conditioning is primarily understanding and wanting. This will take you a long way.

The following paragraph contains a few examples which are always built up in the above mentioned sequence and structure.

The sequence:

1. **Starting situation.**

2. **Analysis of the problem.**

3. **Formulation of objectives.**

4. **Choice of content and organization of the training situation.**

5. **Control and evaluation.**

General measures

- Reduce available space.

- Increase available space.

- More opponents.

- Fewer opponents.

- Force opponent who is not in possession to regain the ball as fast as possible.

- Introduce offside rule.

- Sufficient balls available beside the playing area.

- Only score with headers (only in larger small sided games such as 8 v 8 and 7 v 7 line soccer).

- Set a time limit (e.g. only 5 minutes to go, or last minute).

Effects

- Less time for the players to solve soccer problems.

- More time; longer distances to run and pass.

- Less time, harder to read the game.

- More time, easier to read the game.

- Less time, harder to read the game.

- Less space, less time.

- More continuity, faster resumption of play.

- Play over the flank and lots of heading duels.

- Players are forced to attack more effectively, to win the ball, keep possession of the ball, etc. (depending on the situation).

A few examples:

Example 1:

Preparation for the new season

Conditioning is soccer training.

1. Starting situation:
Players return from vacation and start their preparation for the new season (3 x per week).

2. Analysis of the problem:
The team must be ready to play competitive matches within a few weeks. The players have spent a number of weeks doing nothing and their condition (TIC) therefore falls short of what is needed at this level.

3. Objective:
To develop the players' performance to competitive level, i.e. so that they can tackle and overcome the obstacles they meet at that level (= ability to play 2 x 45 minutes with the aim of winning).

4. Content and organization of the training situation:
Knowledge of conditioning theory, especially elements such as overload, load, and repetition maximum. On the basis of this and other factors, the coach chooses typical soccer drills in which the intensity cannot become too high and which will not tire the players too quickly (players enjoy the drill; sufficient opportunity for recuperation).

Example: small sized games of 5 v 6, or 6 v 6 on a small playing area (1/4 of full-size pitch), with or without full-size goals, small goals and line soccer variants. This form of organization allows the principles of endurance and interval training to be expressed.

This theoretical knowledge is essential to enable coaches to take the correct measures to achieve a set objective on the basis of their observations (players have too much or too little to do, players are gasping for breath, groaning, etc.). For example, the coach may need to change the situation so that more demands are made on the players (e.g. longer or wider playing area, bigger goals, more difficult task).

Besides this main element of conditioning, in the first week all sorts of other elements will be introduced with the aim of improving performance, e.g. physical exercises, stretching exercises, general physical activities such as warming up and cooling down, which the players should eventually be capable of doing without supervision (monitor this). The coach must always be present in order to inject zest, stimulate, give instructions, carry out checks, etc.

In this preseason phase it is certainly important to play a number of genuine practice matches in which the "overload" is too great, e.g. against a team from an older age group. The exertion required will be too much for the not yet conditioned elements, so that an overload is certainly conceivable.

Later in the buildup phase it is advisable to arrange a match in which the players have to draw deep on their reserves. Such a match must be well planned in the context of the whole conditioning package. Pay attention to the work to rest ratio.

5. Control and evaluation

During this preseason phase the coach must observe and listen to the players closely. The coach must indicate whether more or less work can be demanded, from individuals and the team as a whole. He should keep his information up to date in the form of reports, which he should use during the following season.

Practice games are an essential part of the pre-season period.

Example 2:

Pressuring the opposition in order to win the ball (pressing)

1. Starting situation:

In most matches the team finds it difficult to exert pressure on its opponents when it has lost possession, so that it only rarely regains the ball by defending actively. Usually the opposition can build up its moves without hindrance, and the team only regains possession around its own penalty area, as a result of its opponents' mistakes.

2. Analysis of the problem

Most of the players have little idea how a team can work together to regain the ball actively. Some of the players arrive too late, others make unnecessary sliding tackles or commit fouls, while others go after the ball too aggressively and one or two cannot recognize the moment when they have the best chance of succeeding in winning the ball. In short, the team's performance is lacking in this point.

3. Objective:

Developing the idea and the feel for regaining the ball actively. The team must win the ball sooner, further away from its own goal.

4. Content and organization:

The coach must have some knowledge of conditioning theory. The players must experience the problem in an intense form (overload principle) by being exposed to the situation in which it constantly recurs (opposition's buildup). The situation which occurs in a real match is made less complex, easier to "read", clearer.

This is done by reducing the number of players involved. This lets players "feel" who is doing things wrong, how everyone is helping, or not helping, each other, who can't keep up with the pace, etc. Such flaws are shown up more intensely.

A drill is chosen in which 4 attackers face 3 defenders, with the attackers trying to score past a goalkeeper in a full-size goal.

The attackers start near the center circle and the playing area is as wide as the penalty area. The 3 defenders try to challenge for the ball as fast and actively as possible, without neglecting their defensive task (= preventing goals). The task of the 3 defenders is very difficult in terms of:

• being able to read situations;
• making the right choices;
• communicating with each other;
• taking instructions from others;
• fulfilling their task, even when they are very tired.

This means that after a few attacking or defensive actions, the players need a lot of time to recover. During this time the coach can give a few general or personal instructions and the players should stretch and relax (acceleration of recovery). We find that the work periods must be relatively short in this form of comparable small sized games (5 v 4, 6 v 5 or 7 v 6 on a full-size pitch), and that its intensity must be similar to that experienced during a genuine competitive match, i.e. full effort, motivation and concentration.

The objective of the game must be clear - to win the ball and play it to a striker, for example - because only then will the players give full effort and concentration.

For this problem, other variations can be chosen in the practice situation, e.g. all sorts of variations of line soccer, and a 1 v 1 drill may provide the essential reference points for dealing with the shortcomings

of individual players (elements of technique and insight). The physical capabilities of individuals play a key role in this type of drill. A game of 1 v 1 cannot be kept up for too long, and a period of rest must be incorporated after each situation.

Time for a much needed rest and an assessment of whether the objective has been achieved.

5. Control and evaluation:

The elements which have been handled during training sessions will have to be tested again in a competitive situation. The coach has to find out whether everyone understands the idea, the objective. When he coaches during a competitive game he will have to provide his players with feedback on this aspect. The players need to hear from the coach when the moment was right to pressure the ball, who has to provide cover, who dove in too quickly, and exactly why they should hold off. In short, the players' condition must have improved in this area after a few training sessions.

This means that they must be able to carry out their task better and more effectively.

CHAPTER 12
TASKS AND FUNCTIONS

Positional systems

People often talk about 4-3-3, 4-4-2 or 3-4-3 formations. Each tactical system of play and its associated positional system has its advantages and disadvantages. The important thing is that each player must be familiar with the task he has to carry out in his given position.

As long as everyone can carry out his task properly, the choice of tactics depends on aspects such as the impor- tance of the game (in youth soccer the important factor is the development of the players), the weather conditions, the team's position in the league table, etc. Usually, however, the skills and abilities of a team's players will dictate the tactics which suit it best.

How the players translate the chosen tactics into practice depends on their insight into the game. The players must have sufficient skills, insight and commu- nicative ability to be able to implement the tactics.

Tactics start with the team formation, i.e. the positional system. This depends on the abilities of the available players. A team may sometimes decide to modify its formation in view of what the coach knows about the tactics of the opposing team. This will not often be the case in youth soccer.

The best positional system comprises the goalkeeper, a sweeper, three defend- ers, three midfielders and three attackers (i.e. a 4-3-3 or 3-4-3, depending on whether the sweeper plays in front of or behind the three defenders).

The coach must be familiar with the tasks and functions associated with this formation. This chapter is based on the style of play of most club teams in the Netherlands. It is important that each player is aware of his objectives (what is expected of him in his position) and how they are to be realized in the context of the team as a whole, the lines that make up the team, and the individuals who make up the lines.

Every task has its own specific requirements.

Important elements are:
- Basic formation.
- Description of objectives:
  - team as a whole;
  - lines that make up the team;
  - positions that make up the lines.
- Distinguishing between:
  a. when the team is in possession;
  b. when the opposition is in possession.

A team's tactics are based on two central principles:

1. **The result:**
   the objective of playing soccer is to win.

2. **Enjoyment of the game.**

The constructive, attacking, forward-oriented attitude has an important place in the way youngsters play soccer. Winning (the ultimate objective) with it, however, is a different matter. From the age of about 13, the outcome of players' actions are the most important factor. The players must subsequently learn to put the performance of the team as a whole above their individual performances (16 - 18 years).

This is only possible if the players understand their tasks, both individually and in the context of the team as a whole. In youth soccer the players' development takes precedence over winning the championship. The coach therefore has a different objective (teaching his players how to win) than the players, who certainly regard the championship as their main objective. High demands are made on the players. Their performance during the actual match reveals whether they can satisfy them or not.

The following questions are answered during the actual match:

1. Was the objective achieved? (Did the team get a good result?)

2. Did the player understand his task? (Did he read the game?)

3. Did the player carry out his task well? (Can he do it?)

4. Is there good cooperation, sufficient balance, sufficient communication?

In general:
For a team to be able to implement the chosen tactics, the coach must devote sufficient attention to them in discussions, training sessions, and post-match talks.

A clear explanation of the tasks must be hammered home, over and over again.

The following points must be repeatedly hammered home:

- The formation, the positional system, who plays where.

- The tactics (how to buildup, attack, defend; who does what in the various situations).

- Tasks and responsibilities associated with the various positions (individual and as part of a line and the team as a whole).

- The quality of positional play must become a matter of routine, which the whole team must work at and try to perfect (insight into the objectives of positional play).

- Winning 1 v 1 duels.

- The yield in the final phase of positional play (are scoring chances created through the middle and/or over the flanks?)

Basic formation, standard structure

1 Goalkeeper

3 Sweeper
2 Right Full-back   4 Stopper   5 Left Full-back

6 Right Mid-fielder   7 Center Midfielder   8 Left Mid-fielder

6 Right Forward   10 Striker   11 Left Forward

To learn how to coach, you need to learn to read the game.

The whole team

In possession (buildup/attack)

- The emphasis is on positional play, the quality of the positional play, the rhythm of the positional play.

- The main objective is to play the ball forward.

- The formation of the team is important, especially the distances between the players down the center and on the flanks (not to short, not too long).

- Positional play requires unbroken concentration and alertness (stay involved, with and without the ball).

- Aim for perfection in routine actions: no bad passes, no unnecessary loss of possession, no unnecessary runs, correct ball speed, accuracy, etc.

- A lot of effort (positional play) must be put into creating a few chances.

Through proper positional play the ball must eventually be played deep.

- When the ball is regained after pressuring the opposition, do not try anything too hastily; a different sort of concentration is needed, so resist being too aggressive, and don't play any bad passes (switch of mode).

- Then cross the ball, move around in the penalty area, get sufficient players involved, don't wait, look for opportunities.

- If opponents fall back, exercise more patience in buildup (don't succumb to the temptation to hit a long ball if it is not really on).

- Keep looking for chances to play the ball forward, don't get bogged down in `endless square passing (concentrate on the final third of the pitch).

- Communication between the player on the ball and the players upfront.

- Principle of attacking is over the flanks.

- The 6 players (2,3,4,5,6,8) behind the 3 forwards must create chances for the 3 attackers (supporting players).

Opponents in possession (defending/disrupting the opposition's buildup)

- Objective: to regain the ball as quickly as possible, and as far away from the team's own goal as possible. This requires: good organization, understanding, insight and concentration from all players.

  1. The strikers are needed - wingers fall back and squeeze opponents out towards the sideline.
  - Support teammates who are pressuring the opposition (6,7, and 8).
  - Take up the right position (some times a few yards can make a big difference).

2. Support from the back; 3 defenders + 1 sweeper.
   - Stay close to the man in possession and don't allow him to get past.
   - Chain reaction: at the right moment one player challenges for the ball; his teammates must follow up; the first two might just fail to win the ball but the third or fourth will succeed.
   - Force opposition to stay away from goal as much as possible.
   - The opposition's buildup play is the platform for a counter attack; opponents are in attacking positions and are therefore vulnerable to a well timed counter.
   - 1 v 1 situations must be exploited: regain the ball, close down opponent's options, lure opponent into a trap and then strike.

- Defend as far upfield as possible.
- Reach agreements on offside.
- Fore-checking before the center line (near center circle)
- In general: each player should take up position as far upfield as possible and pick up opponents as they enter his zone without the ball.
- Fall back to the center circle/center line or try to pin the opposition down immediately.
- All players join in - whole team switches rapidly.
- The right moment to go for the ball is when the opposition plays a long ball, especially if it is not accurate (close down "escape routes" in the immediate vicinity of the ball).
- Sequence for regaining the ball:
  - Routines (taking up position, closing down space, dropping back).
  - Pressing by midfielders and defenders (accelerating, closing down).
  - Challenging.
  - Chasing the ball.

- Winning the ball.

- Don't always challenge and chase at top speed. Wait for the right moment, then go all-out. Take the initiative if you can force an opponent into a difficult position (e.g. towards weaker flank or player).

We did it. . . . !

Tasks of the various lines

Defense

1

3

2   4   5

In possession (buildup/attack)
- No unnecessary loss of possession.
- Move the ball quickly, switch the play quickly.
- Avoid mistakes in buildup play.
- Good positional play, make the best use of the available space (also with respect to opponent's strikers).
- Always aim to put one or more teammates into space.
- Communicate with each other, instruct each other.

Midfield

7

6   8

- Control the ball in your own zone, don't go forward too soon, retain formation.
- No unnecessary loss of possession, no unnecessary runs with the ball.
- Support the three strikers.

Attack

9   11

10

- 3 forwards.
- Take up optimal formation (create as much space as possible).
- Central striker (10) must not set off too early for long pass.
- The individual skills of these 3 attackers are very important in this tactical system. These skills are an important weapon but also involve an element of risk.
- Four players should push up into the penalty area when a cross comes in. (i.e. cross from 11 -> 10, 9, 7 and 6 make runs into penalty area)
- Good communication with the players involved in the buildup. "Read" the buildup play, anticipate the long ball, and try to create the most favorable conditions for taking a pass if it should come.

Opposition in possession (Defending, disrupting the opposition's buildup)

Defense

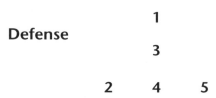

- Communication and instruction with regard to what you see (takeover, switch, offside, etc.).
- The closer to goal, the closer the marking from 2, 4, and 5.
- Ensure that the sweeper (3) is not drawn into 1 v 1 situations -> this is the responsibility of the other defenders and the midfielders.
- Defend sensibly - don't give away free-kicks.
- "Crowd" your opponent skillfully with out conceding free-kicks.

Midfield

7

6   8

- The two wide midfielders (6 and 8) must play a controlling role; they should not go too far forward, and in general, should not overrun their wingers.
- Defend cleverly and sensibly, without committing dumb fouls; remain poised.
- It causes problems, if 1 of the 3 midfielders fails to mark tightly. The opponent has the opportunity to escape.
- Don't be bypassed too easily, maintain pressure on opponent.
- Use your body.
- Don't dive in, keep your opponent in front of you.
- Link well with strikers (proper spacing between the lines). Cover the man in

In order to win the game, the tasks and manning of positions must be clear.

your zone and go with him as long as he is in your zone.

- "Squeezing" (= giving cover or closing down space to the side where the ball is). Squeezing by wide midfielders (6 and 8) when opposition builds up or attacks down the other flank.

Attack

9   11

10

- Fall back to just short of or beyond the center line in the opposition's buildup phase.

- Stay in contact with each other, try to take up good positions (push towards the flank where the ball is).

- Close down opponent's buildup options and prevent long balls forward.

- Choose the right moment to chase after the ball.

- The 3 strikers (9, 10, and 11) must cover the opposition's 4 defenders.

Individual tasks per position

In possession (buildup/attack)

1 goalkeeper
- Remain involved in positional play.
- Good restart by means of pass, throw, kick, goal-kick.
- Good communication with teammates.

1 sweeper
- Take control.
- Switch the play; aim to play the ball forward and push up whenever possible.
- Regulate ball circulation.

3 defenders (left, right and central)
- Move out when in possession to facilitate the buildup play (important role in positional play) - draw strikers away, create space.

Good communication is necessary during restarts.

2 controlling midfielders (left and right)
- Good positional play especially in relation to wingers, defenders and sweeper.
- When attacks are developed down the other flank, push up into the penalty area at the last moment (heading power).
- Switch play from the center to the flanks and vice versa; no risky square passes.
- Don't run too much with the ball (out of position + big risk of losing possession).
- Avoid overrunning the winger too often and crowding his space.

1 central midfielder
- Play in support of central striker.
- Don't play too far forward (think about the space behind you + switch play/send ball through to left and right flanks).
- Good positional play in building up attacks.
- Getting into scoring positions.
- Scoring goals.

2 wingers (left and right)
- Come in on crosses from the other flank (header) -> don't stay out on the wing -> come inside.
- Result from crosses is important, ball must arrive in front of goal.
- Good communication, especially in final phase when cross has to be made.
- Scoring goals.

1 central striker
- Scoring goals.
- Getting into scoring positions.
- Working hard to get into positions to take long balls.
- "Reading" the buildup play.

Opposition in possession (Defending, disrupting the opposition's buildup)

1 goalkeeper
- Preventing goals.
- Keep moving, concentrate.
- "Read" the situation.
- Aim to get off the line when opponents hit long balls forward ((sweeper role/close down space).
- Organize the defensive line.

1 sweeper
- Preventing goals.
- Take control/read the game -> through "free" role
- Give cover.
- Close down space at right moment when opposition hits a long forward pass (anticipate this moment in opposition's buildup).

3 defenders (left, right and central)
- Preventing goals.
- The closer to goal, the closer the marking.
- Regulate offside trap (don't hang back).
- Mark inside.
- Squeeze/give cover.
- Be very alert in 1 v 1 situations; not simply aggressive, but also technically accomplished; don't dive in, keep your man in front of you, don't give away free-kicks.
- It is essential to be aggressive but not to the extent of conceding free-kicks.

1 central midfielder
- Controlling task, so keep things in equilibrium, don't play too far forward.
- Pick up any unmarked opponent who pushes up.

2 controlling midfielders (left and right)
- Think defensively, play well in your own zone, close down opponent's space (prevent forward pass).
- Supporting role.
- Join in when pressure is being exerted on the ball, don't offer any chance of escape.

2 wingers
- Not only responsible for their own markers (fullbacks), but must also defend space in midfield, "squeeze" inside, and follow their own markers back when they push forward.
- Prevent opponent (fullback) participating in opposition's buildup down the flank; prevent long ball being played forward.
- "Squeeze" inside when opposition builds up over the other flank or through the middle.
- If other players are more dangerous than the direct opponent, pick them up, e.g. if the central striker stays upfield and the opposing central defender pushes forward.
- Cut out crosses.

1 central, advanced striker
- In close cooperation with his two wingers, disrupt opposition's buildup, prevent opposition from playing the ball out.
- Choose the right moment to challenge for the ball.
- Don't chase too much on your own.
- Keep opponent in front of you in order to give your wingers time to close up in support.

Every player is involved, everybody has a task to perform.

CHAPTER 13

YOUTH PLAYERS WITHIN
THE SOCCER CLUB

This chapter deals with the place of youngsters within a soccer club.

The foundation of youth soccer

Some 400,000 boys and girls between the ages of 6 and 18 currently play soccer in the Netherlands. The structure of youth soccer in the Netherlands is illustrated by the pyramid shown below. A list of questions follow, aimed at helping club officials to analyze how their clubs can give shape to the various aspects of the "foundation" of youth soccer.

A. Organization

- Is there special attention for each age group?
- Are the players given a say in their own affairs, and assigned responsibilities?
- Does the club have a youth policy?

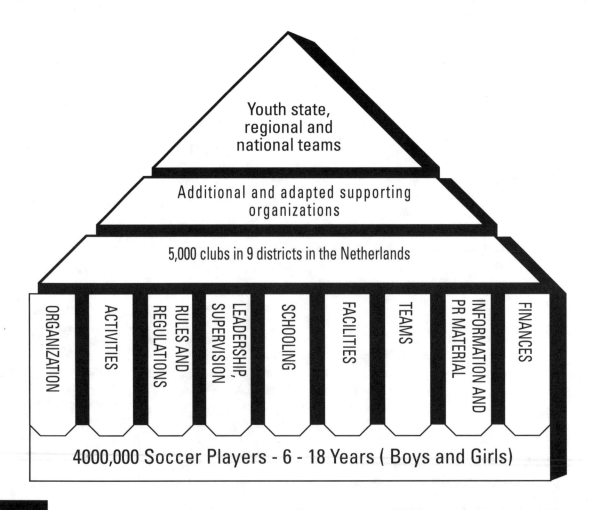

Youth state, regional and national teams

Additional and adapted supporting organizations

5,000 clubs in 9 districts in the Netherlands

ORGANIZATION

ACTIVITIES

RULES AND REGULATIONS

LEADERSHIP, SUPERVISION

SCHOOLING

FACILITIES

TEAMS

INFORMATION AND PR MATERIAL

FINANCES

4000,000 Soccer Players - 6 - 18 Years (Boys and Girls)

B. Activities

- How often do the players train, and how often do they play?
- What is the quality of the training/coaching?
- What other activities (besides training sessions and matches) are provided for the players?
- Can the players use the club's premises and equipment freely, e.g. to play "street soccer"?
- What activities are carried out which are aimed at ensuring support and continuity within the youth section.

C. Rules and regulations

- Are the rules of play sufficiently adapted to the various age groups?
- Are they applied as such?
- Can exceptions be made? Is good use made of this option by the club, and the various governing bodies of soccer?
- Are the youngsters themselves adequately consulted before changes are made to the rules and regulations?
- Are the youngsters' interests taken into account when contracts are written with sponsors?

Youngs players need different rules!

D. Leadership and supervision

- Are all activities sufficiently supervised?
- Are the supervisors adequately qualified?
- Are the players encouraged to contribute?

E. Schooling

- Is the club aware of the available courses and does it make use of them? (Refereeing courses, coaching courses, etc.)
- Does the club organize its own courses?
- Do the players contribute to them?
- Is there any form of schooling fund? Could a sponsor be found for this?

F. Facilities

- Are the club's training/game facilities sufficiently adapted to youngsters' needs? (Dimensions of the pitches and goals, height of clothing hangers, showers, notice board, etc.)
- Are balls and equipment available which are suitable for use by youngsters?
- Does the clubhouse offer suitable accommodation for the youngsters or is it little more than a bar?
- Are there sufficient accommodations for boys and girls?
- Can the players use the training facilities all year round?
- Does the club have its own gymnasium?

G. Team selection and scouting

- How does the selection procedure work for the youth players within the club?
- At what age are the players first evaluated in terms of their soccer performance?
- What selection criteria are applied? (Technique, insight, communication.)

- Do the players who don't make the first team of their age group still receive good quality coaching?
- What level of support is available for players who are dropped from a first team?
- What level of support is there for representative teams?

H. Information, PR and Publicity

- Is there an information bulletin for informing all club members about club activities? Is it written in a form which youngsters can also read easily?
- Are new members informed properly about the club's style?
- Can the players express their ideas, wishes, grievances and suggestions in the club journal?

I. Finances

- Is it clear where the club spends its money?
- What are the players' contributions used for? Can this be demonstrated?
- Does the youth section have its own budget?
- Are qualified personnel assigned to the players? (Coaches, supervisors, etc.)
- Are the club's financial resources distributed evenly over the various sections (seniors, juniors, beginners) in terms of expenditure on personnel, training sessions, equipment, etc., on the basis of the principle of equal treatment.

J. Other club activities

- What is the relationship between out door and indoor soccer within the club?
- Is there a good balance between recreational, and performance-related soccer activities?

- Are additional activities organized, e.g. participation in international tournaments, training camps, etc.
- Does the club publicize its membership figures, sponsorship deals, etc.
- Is there additional support for top players with regard to their education, etc.

Top

The top of the pyramid is formed by the club's first teams (under 13 through under 18 teams). Some of these players will be members of representative teams, e.g. state, regional, or even national teams. The diagram makes clear that the foundations of the pyramid must be strong if it is to have a good top.

A club which ensures that it has strong foundations is more likely to supply members of representative teams, and to generate a steady flow of talented youngsters through its own ranks. A club which wants to operate a good youth policy can start by answering the questions listed above.

This means that choices must be made. These choices will have financial consequences, e.g. with respect to the salaries of the coaches, etc.

Unusual footwear.

Minority groups

This is not the place for a detailed treatment of this subject. However, the soccer world has proved that it can integrate players from minority groups with great success. This is clear at all levels of the game.

Youngsters who play soccer in the Netherlands come from a wide range of cultural and ethnic backgrounds. The best evidence of their successful integration is the Dutch national team.

The purpose of playing soccer is to have fun together and to play competitive matches. This objective transcends such factors as skin color, cultural background, religious belief, sex and disposition.

The Dutch Soccer Association is concerned with the sport of soccer. Any sporting body, in this case the soccer association, must ensure that:

a. the sport is played;

b. the sport is learned;

c. the sport generates pleasure.

Soccer brings people together.
Just as in other sectors of society:
There are no problems, simply people.

Total emancipation: players from a minority group, female too, and twins!

Recruiting

New players can be recruited from youngsters who have not yet decided to play a particular sport. Between the ages of 6 and 16 both boys and girls can be targeted.

A club may also wish to focus on the handicapped, or on minority groups. Familiarization activities can be organized in cooperation with the teaching staff of local schools.

An example

A Dutch local authority organizes an annual spring tournament for children who attend the 6 local primary schools.

The competition lasts two days. Mixed teams from the various age groups play 7-a-side on half of a full sized pitch.

Other activities include penalty shooting, exhibitions of various skills, etc. More than 300 players, including 100 girls, participated when the tournament was held for the first time in 1985.

The number of participants has increased from year to year, and it is estimated that 35% of the pupils are involved. This is a relatively high figure for such events.

Do such activities yield new members? The answer is yes, but only if there is good follow-up, e.g. giving the players the chance to join in the club's training sessions.

Conditions for a successful activity:

- Good preparation.

- Appoint a work group, with clearly defined individual responsibilities.

- Draw up a plan and stick to it.

- Consult school directors in advance (agree dates).

- Consider cooperation with other sports clubs.

- Organization must be perfect on the day.

- Take parents, teachers, cafeteria facilities, possibility of bad weather, etc. into consideration.

- Plan follow-up activities.

- Evaluate the event afterwards with a view to identifying any improvements which could be made next time.

Pleasure, allied with concentration and attention to the coach.

Club policy is youth policy

The staff of the Dutch Soccer Association has worked hard to improve youth soccer in recent years.

This book is one of the results of their work. In our opinion, all those who feel themselves responsible for the sport of soccer should help to improve youth soccer. It may be a cliché that the future belongs to the young, but it is nevertheless true.

The club has some work to do before this girl can play properly.

The youth coordinator

A number of initiatives have been taken to spread these ideas among the clubs.

It was apparent the lines of communication between the Dutch Soccer Association and the clubs were too long and included too many links. The more links there are, the greater the chance that one of them will fail. As a result, important information often does not get through to the enthusiastic (and voluntary) youth staff at the club.

We all want young players to be able to progress successfully. This is why the Dutch Soccer Association is encouraging clubs to appoint coaching coordinators. This is nothing new, but it is very necessary for any club which recognizes the importance of its young soccer players.

A coaching coordinator is not only needed to facilitate shorter lines of communication. He also has an important role in representing the interests of youth soccer within the club. He is responsible for all technical aspects, from the sort of balls used to the types of 4 v 4 games played, from ensuring continuity in the training of youth coaches to organizing information evenings for team managers.

He must be an intermediary between the club management and the player aspects (youth management, staff, coaches, parents). He must also handle contacts with the world outside the club.

Such contacts may be with the full-time coaches of the Dutch Soccer Association (concerning matters such as 4 v 4, staff training, state, regional and national youth teams, etc.), other clubs (tournaments, cooperation, etc.) or schools (school soccer, promotional activities, etc.).

In short, it is clear that the youth coordinator must have the technical background to ensure that he can achieve his objective, i.e. improving the learning climate for young players within the club.

Communications with the clubs have been greatly improved in recent years by means of instructional seminars, regional seminars, courses for youth coaches and target-group seminars (e.g. girls' and women's soccer).

The Dutch Soccer Association aims to make use of the bonds it has forged with the clubs. This can be done most successfully when the youth coordinator function is fulfilled by someone who is already familiar with the working of the club and the Dutch Soccer Association. The job is certainly demanding.

Youngsters also follow the performance of the under 18 team.

The status of the coaching coordinator is comparable to that of the coaching director. Many clubs are willing to spend the necessary money, because they now recognize the justice of this comparison, not only in terms of the time required to do the job, but above all in terms of the required quality of the work.

Profile of a coaching coordinator

Facilitates good communications between the soccer players and the Dutch Soccer Association, so that the information intended to improve soccer as a product also reaches its intended target, i.e. the players.

The responsibilities are:

- Support the Dutch Soccer Association's youth selection procedures

- Organization of 4 v 4 tournaments

- Organization of soccer camps /soccer days

- Promoting participation by youth coaches, team managers, volunteers, and referees in specific educational courses

- Distribution of promotional material produced by the Dutch Soccer Association and the club.

- Organization of "theme" evenings for the players, possibly in cooperation with the Dutch Soccer Association

- Distribution of the Dutch Soccer Association's information on youth soccer to those involved

- Promotion of girls soccer

The coaching coordinator should preferably have been a player and a qualified coach.

Fair-play: time for..... soccer quality

There can be a world of difference between two soccer matches. One can have the fans on the edge of their seats because of the attractive attacking play, excitement, enjoyment, effort and, not least, the respect prevailing between the two teams. In another game, the limit of each team's ambition may be to avoid defeat, so they take no risks and are happy with a score of 0 - 0. In such a comparison it isn't hard to decide where the best soccer was played. But in other cases it can be more difficult to say who had the best of the game. The best team may not always win, because soccer is not that predictable.

And what is attractive soccer?

Can a team which aims to defend in depth and wait for opportunities to launch fast counter attacks be described as attractive?

A game can be said to be full of good soccer if it contains lots of exciting combinations and individual runs, but what if all this fine play doesn't result in goals? Even attractive soccer can be ultimately boring if it doesn't yield goalscoring opportunities. A sports journalist once wrote that the game "died of its own beauty" after watching the Brazilian national team in the 1960s.

The quality of soccer can be evaluated in many different ways. There is nothing wrong with this. Differences of opinion can stimulate soccer development, provided they are expressed clearly. Clearly formulated opinions are a good basis for seeking areas of agreement.

Analyzes of the quality of a game (= the level of fair play) can only be viewed in the context of winning and losing. The analysis involves evaluating the process by which the result is achieved. The better the game is played (in accordance with the original initial objective of the game), the more safeguards will have to be built in to achieve a positive result.

The various playing concepts must be viewed within this context. Such concepts are designed to enable a team to exploit its strengths (the skills of its players) and cover its weaknesses in the interest of winning the match. An analysis should not include generalities which bear little or no relationship to the players' actions.

For example, players may be said to have shown too much respect for the

Collisions are sometimes inevitable.

opposition, or to be worried about their health. It is better to look at the degree to which a team is capable of playing in accordance with the original objective of the game: the desire to attack, the ability to gain the ball within the rules of the game, and the ability to restart the buildup when the ball has been regained.

A foul results in a free-kick for the opposition, and this certainly doesn't help a team to attain its objective. A team must be in possession before it can build up, attack, and score! Players appreciate this point.

It is important that players appreciate why committing a foul is not a good idea when viewed in the light of the objective "winning the game".

Team selection

Selecting players is often a problem, especially if the selection criteria have not been clearly defined. The comments below are intended to help coaches in this respect.

Why select players?

The better players should play with and against each other.

The aim of selecting players for various teams is to give them the opportunity to develop at their own level.

The better players play alongside and against each other. Matches which are challenging for all players are matches at a level which the players can only just achieve. Such matches stimulate them to improve their performance.

A player who finds himself at too low a level becomes bored, and a player who finds himself at too high a level comes under so much pressure that he has no chance to develop.

In both cases the player doesn't learn anything, and his development may even go backwards.

- Players at too low a level: are too lazy, move the ball too slowly, switch too slowly from defense to attack and vice versa, don't play directly enough, don't bother to read the game, etc.

- Players at too high a level: keep running after their opponents, make too many (badly timed) sliding tackles, grab their opponent's shirt, etc. instead of solving problems in line with the objectives of the game.

This is connected with enjoyment of the game. As has already been stated in this book, players must enjoy soccer if they are to have the right motivation to learn. Each player must therefore be addressed at his own level.

The best players should play alongside and against each other from the time when they reach an age at which their enjoyment becomes connected with winning and success.

This generally occurs between the ages of 10 and 12. If a club starts to select players at a younger age, i.e. in the interests of the club or the parents or the coach rather than those of the player, this can harm the enjoyment of both selected and non-selected players. They are not yet ready for this step.

It should perhaps be remarked here that clubs in the Netherlands can field mixed teams of boys and girls up to the age of 14, and mixed teams of 15 and 16 year-olds are permitted if special permission is obtained.

The considerations mentioned above also apply to girls. It often happens that a girl of, for example, 14 is pushed into the women's team, either because she is very talented or because the team "can certainly use her". Again, this can harm the development of such a child. The individual development of talented youngsters should take precedence over the interests of the club. The interests of the girl would be best served by leaving her in her own age group team.

Scouting: what to look for?

Scouting within the club (following the players' progress with a view to integrat-

ing them into the club's first teams at the various age groups) should be approached seriously and carefully. For the players themselves, the prospect of playing in a club team is important, a target to aim at.

Careful scouting must take account of the following:

• What criteria are applied to assessing a talented player?
• What age group are we looking at?
• What period are we looking at? (All categories or a specific age group.)

Scouts should be involved in discussions on the following:

• The objective of the club's team selection policies, and the manner of implementing them (an important means of promoting the development of young soccer players).
• Criteria to be applied to the scouting of talented young players (in relation to their age).
• The place and function of competitive leagues for young players.

Objectives of selected teams

Everyone knows that a player of 10 cannot be expected to perform as well as a player who is in the under 16 Team. The question is: what can, and what can't, be expected of young players?

The objectives associated with the activities of the youngest selected teams (10-12 years old) have more to do with developing basic aspects of playing soccer (technical skills, insight, vision) coupled with specific characteristics which are typical of the age group. The objectives with older teams are to develop collective technical and tactical skills and aspects which help to win matches.

Intelligence and soccer

It is interesting to include the intellectual qualities of young soccer players in discussions on soccer talent. What is more important: a player's general intelligence, as reflected in his IQ, or specific physical characteristics and skills which play a key role in the context of soccer?

Consideration could be given to a player's powers of observation (Does he grasp things quickly? Does he pick out the essential features? Does he recognize soccer situations quickly? Can he anticipate his teammates' intentions?) and how he recognizes and interprets what he observes.

Observation and recognition are the driving forces in the playing of soccer. Things are different in track, for example, where the starter's gun is the decisive factor. The creation of a soccer climate or atmosphere, a climate of success, is the first requisite for the development of young soccer players and hence for spotting talented young players, because this is the ideal environment in which their talents can blossom.

The ambition of every player: to play for a professional team.

The tasks of the club are, above all:

- to ensure participation in good competitions;
- to ensure that there are adequate training opportunities at the club;
- to support players who are invited to play for state, regional, or national teams;
- to provide good coaching, adapted to the children's ages.

What makes a good scout?

A good scout must have a good soccer brain. Considerable experience of the world of soccer is essential.
It has been said that:

> *"Even a groundskeeper can be a good scout - but he must have been a groundskeeper for a long time!"*

The essential thing is to be familiar with how youngsters play soccer, how they enjoy it and what they want from it (and a groundskeeper has probably observed more youth soccer games than most).

Scouting in practice

In practice, scouting comes down to observing how young players solve soccer problems:

- What qualities do players demonstrate, what talent do they have for solving soccer problems?

- What potential do players demonstrate for making the largest possible contribution to winning a game?

- Can players solve soccer problems within the confines of the specific task associated with their position in the team? (See Chapter 12: "Tasks and functions within the team".)

Criteria were formerly applied which gave little insight into the soccer ability of a player. All kinds of aspects such as running speed, physical stature, height, jumping power, running style, technical skills, and mental characteristics such as drive and competitive ruthlessness were considered, but they are poor pointers to a player's capacities in a real soccer situation. And that is what is really important: what a player demonstrates in a soccer match. We now talk about soccer ability rather than stamina, strength, speed, suppleness, mentality, etc.

Players were often assessed primarily on the basis of physical factors. In youth soccer, however, the development process of the players must always be borne in mind (growth spurts, ability to withstand stress at a certain age, social development, schools, etc.). The most important factor is therefore whether players demonstrate that they have grasped the game and have understood and seen its objectives. This is the basis of their actions, and a scout bases his evaluation of their talents on these actions.

In practice it can be seen that there is no typical "ideal" way of solving soccer problems, nor is there a typical "ideal" soccer player. Players must carry out a task by making the best use of their own talents, and these differ widely from player to player. A scout will look at how a young player handles his task in general terms (e.g. "He can tackle well"), but will look at an older player in more detail (e.g. "He wins the ball well, stays on his feet, and switches quickly from defense to attack").

The selection criteria are based on the realization of the previously described playing objectives in the three main moments of the game, and the associated general premises. Above all the main objective -> winning the game - must be kept in view.

The will to win - an important selection criteria.

A few examples:

When a player operates in defense and always chooses the best option when he has the ball, but makes a number of mistakes in performing his main task, i.e. defending (= preventing the opposition from scoring goals), then he is unsuited to that task and a scout will reject him as a defender. It may be that he can develop further or be converted to another position.

If a very small, fragile midfielder hardly ever wins a race for the ball or a tackle but demonstrates good passing ability in creating chances for the strikers and playing the ball into space, it is clear that he can fulfill an important creative role in the midfield buildup. Other players will have to provide balance by taking over the other facets of midfield play. Players of this type are especially deserving of a chance to develop at a higher level.

Selection activities:

It was once thought (especially in eastern European countries) that special exercises could be developed to determine whether or not a player was talented. Batteries of tests were often developed (and still are in, for example, Austria and Switzerland), involving all sorts of physical exercises as well as drills for demonstrating ball skills.

The most important aspect in this activity is ignored, namely that observation is the basis of playing soccer.

A player is selected on the basis of his performance in his club.

The players therefore sprint for the sake of sprinting, jump for the sake of jumping, juggle the ball in the air for the sake of juggling the ball in the air, and shoot hard for the sake of shooting hard. This has nothing to do with what happens on the pitch during a real game (goal-orientedness, use of technique to score a goal, etc.).

If an extra selection activity has to be carried out, it must be done on the basis of typical soccer situations, which must be organized and regulated in such a way as to throw light on the contribution the players make towards winning a match. For example a one against one situation with one player attacking and one defending a goal, or small sided games (4 v 4 and variations).

It should be clear that talent spotting is not such a simple matter. The very best players will always rise to the top, so they are not the problem; such players usually come forward at a very early stage. The difficulty is to assess the potential of players who are not quite capable of matching the very best but who will later make up the majority of the team.

The Dutch Youth Plan

Talented club players are considered for selection for representative teams of the Dutch Soccer Association. This is the second step on the way to the top.

For almost 25 years, a system has been in place in the Netherlands for finding and scouting talented young players, selecting them for representative youth teams, and coaching and grooming them in such a way that the very best of them end up in representative national teams. This is the Dutch Youth Plan.

Some 20 professional coaches are employed by the Dutch Soccer Association to help implement this plan. They are responsible for spotting, selecting and coaching talented youngsters (girls and boys) in the age groups "Under 13, 14, 15 and 16" (boys) and "Under 13, 14, 16 and 18" (girls).

Each year 16 players are selected in each age group in 20 districts in the Netherlands. This means 20 x 16 = 320 talented players in each age group.

National youth squads

These young players participate in training sessions and also play competitive games against the other district teams. The coaches have the task of noting and monitoring the best players in these games and forwarding their names to the staff of the Dutch Soccer Association. The coaches also maintain contacts with the many amateur and professional clubs in the districts.

Full concentration is demanded from players of a selected state team.

Boys and girls play soccer together

Youngsters judge each other mainly on the basis of personal experience, irrespective of their sex and existing prejudices. Mixed soccer has brought about a reversal in the approach to boys and girls.

Boys and girls in the Netherlands can compete in mixed teams up to the age of 14, or even 16 if special permission is obtained. It is noticeable that existing prejudices soon disappear or are put into perspective when boys and girls play soccer together.

The spirit that prevails in mixed teams depends not on the sex of the players but on their individual talents. Players of both sexes are judged only on their soccer ability. No one says "Girls can't play soccer but boys can" any longer. Without exception the girls are able to match the boys, also in their physical performance.

As Pauline, a 13 year-old girl in a mixed team, says: "If you have played soccer for a long time, as I have with the boys, there is no difference. We are just as tough, and just as good as they are; we are all on the same level."

Differences in physique between boys and girls first begin to appear around the age of 15.

Girls' soccer tends to support existing prejudices rather than banish them. Girls who only play soccer alongside and against girls all agree that boys are generally better soccer players. Girls in mixed teams have a more positive image of themselves and are more aware of their potential.

The same phenomenon can be observed among coaches. Coaches of mixed teams are more cautious in their judgments. "Boys could learn a lot from the girls' discipline and willingness to learn. It is good for boys and girls to play soccer together."

Improved behavior

Finally it appears that boys and girls also behave better off the pitch. Boys in particular are suddenly more socially inclined, both on and off the field, according to the girls.

Girls therefore make a contribution to youngsters' (soccer) development in general. It used to be feared that the boys would in general be less well prepared for their soccer future, but now boys and girls profit from each other's talents and acquire a broader and richer outlook on people.

The Dutch Soccer Association is of the opinion that youngsters assume that everyone must be able to do what he or she wants to. And that is progress in comparison with the situation 10 years ago.

Youngsters must be confronted with each other's talents in mixed groups in order to see the potential that exists in each individual.

This is nothing new of course. In the Netherlands this philosophy has made separate boys' and girls' schools a thing of the past.

Mixed soccer has a positive effect on the (soccer) development of boys and girls.

Mixed soccer: the facts

On average:

- No difference in aptitude or talent between girls and boys, men and women.

- No difference in the capabilities of children aged up to 12 years:
  - physically;
  - mentally;
  - socially.

- 12-14 age group:
  Girls are stronger, faster, bigger, heavier than boys.

- 14-16 age group:
  Boys become stronger, faster, bigger and heavier than girls at about the age of 15.

- Mixed soccer is good for the general and soccer development of boys and girls, because they both contribute their own values.

- The decision to allow girls to play alongside and against boys was followed by explosive growth in the number of girls playing. This is the basis for the future of girls soccer!

Allowing boys and girls to play mixed soccer in the 14-16 age group is, however, controversial.

The arguments which follow are put forward in defense of the case that, in most cases, mixed soccer is beneficial for the development of both boys and girls.

Arguments

Technical

- Girls can play on an equal basis with boys from an early age: girls are often further in their (soccer) development, because girls generally reach puberty before boys.

- Girls of 14 are in a different phase of the soccer learning process than adult women, but are in the same phase as the boys of their age.

The same demands on boys and girls.

- A girl of 14 is not yet ready for women's soccer. In practice, such girls often land in the women's reserve team, and their soccer development suffers (less soccer ability in the team + more physical power means that talented young players cannot develop as well as they might).

- Positive influence on the development of women's soccer at the national and international level. In the important phase between the ages of 14 and 16, talented young players can develop at club level.

- A girl of 14 can always be assigned to a level that corresponds to her abilities, ambitions and enjoyment. She can join a boys under-15 team, or if available a under-18 girls team within the club.

- Because a girl of 14 is, on average, more advanced in her (sport) development than a boy of the same age, she can make a very positive contribution to the development of the boys in her team.

Physical

- Adult female players are, on average, bigger, stronger, faster, heavier, etc. than 14 year-old girls.

- Adults have played sport for more years than 14 year-old girls and therefore have more soccer stamina.

- Girls in the 12-14 age group are, on average, stronger and exhibit more stamina than boys of the same age. The boys make up this difference between their 14th and 16th years.

- Girls of 14 are going through puberty and are not yet fully grown. It is impossible to customize the training and competitive routines of adults to the physical limitations of growing girls. The only options which are available are: skipping a training session, incorporating additional rest periods into a training session, substituting the player (not having her play a full game). This is not good for the physical development of the player (overloads are combated by emergency measures or not recognized, so that injuries occur: muscle injuries, strained tendons and joints, back problems).

An equal duel.

Moreover, the player will spend less time on her soccer (training sessions and matches) than if her training and games were geared to her development phase.

Pedagogic and psychological
- Playing alongside and against each other has a positive influence, in that the child's growing up period is more complete and varied. (Compare the background of co-education, which has resulted in, for example, the disappearance of single-sex schools.

- A child's personal (sport) development with his or her contemporaries proceeds evenly; the child does not need to make forced "jumps" in order to keep up.

- It appears that girls who choose to remain in mixed teams have more definite ideas on what they want to achieve in their sporting and social careers. Such girls often want to go further in their chosen sport. In their hearts they have already decided what they want to do in future.

- Girls who play mixed soccer are more self-confident. They know what they want and don't want, and what they can and can't do. Girls who only play alongside and against other girls have a much more vague image of themselves.

Social
- Passing through the various age group teams with their friends. They belong in the(mixed)team, they feel comfortable.

- Boys and girls from mixed teams have a more factual image of each other. It appears that prejudices have been banished. (The boys and girls judge each other on the basis of their soccer ability and not their sex.)

- Elimination of prejudices in a more balanced atmosphere, so that the emphasis can be placed on other things (focus on team performance instead of individual glory). This can be compared to the process of integration in police forces.

Organizational
- Clubs declare that the girls are team members in their own right. If some of them drop out, there are problems in getting a team together.

- In practice a solution always seems to be found for problems such as showering, etc.

- There may be no women's soccer in the area. In 17 regions of the Netherlands there is no league for the 15-18 age group. Introducing such a league may pose problems. For example, there may not be enough girls in the club to form both a team of 15-18 year-olds and a women's team.

- Questionnaires have shown that many girls stop playing soccer at the age of 14 if they are faced with having to make the step up into women's soccer, although it cannot be said that girls' soccer in the 15-18 age group is stagnating. It can be said that the expansion of mixed soccer can stimulate club membership figures and improve the standard of women's soccer.

ANNEX
DIDACTICS AND METHODOLOGY IN YOUTH SOCCER TRAINING

1. Didactics

Didactics is the science or art of teaching, and this book is concerned with the teaching of soccer.

We learn to play soccer primarily by actually playing. It is therefore important to present the game to players in a way that takes this into account. However, a game of 11 v 11 on a full sized pitch offers few of the opportunities which players need in order to acquire the basics of the game.

In games of 11 v 11, players have too few opportunities to become involved in the game. The situations are too complicated, the players don't properly understand the objectives of the game, and they don't come into contact with the ball often enough.

This is far from ideal, and this is why the staff of the Dutch Soccer Association, the KNVB, decided to make use of a number of practice games (basic games), which emphasize typical elements of "real" soccer, so youngsters can learn how to play.

These games offer the guarantee that:

- The objectives of the game are clear.

- The structure of "real" soccer is still present (the games are played from goal to goal).

- The players are more involved, so they experience the game more intensely.

Another advantage of these simplified soccer games is that once they have started, they can continue indefinitely.

Youngsters keep playing, so there is inevitably lots of repetition (an important aspect of learning).

Each minute of the training session is valuable. The limited time available must be used as efficiently and effectively as possible.

Lots of repetition is necessary at this age.

The players must learn as much as possible. The above mentioned basic games are an important means of learning to play soccer. The coach or supervisor must be able to work with these games. He or she must be capable of using the "learning friendly" characteristics of the basic games to give an extra dimension to the learning process.

Each coach has his own level of aptitude and talent, his own priorities, style and experience. He must also be familiar with a number of rules for coaching and teaching.

You learn to play soccer by actually playing; the coach helps.

These "didactic rules of thumb" give the coach fixed points of reference for coaching in practice. This chapter is concerned with the didactics, i.e. the theory, of teaching and instructing.

The coach, supervisor, etc. should form his own picture of all aspects of the process of teaching young players to play soccer, and all the elements which contribute to its success. All these are dealt with in an ordered sequence.

A coach must be aware of how he instructs and coaches his players. He must constantly ask himself "Am I getting my message across?"

The following aspects are covered:

A. The typical soccer elements which need to be emphasized at the various stages, and the associated questions.

B. A description of a typical situation in daily coaching practice.

These descriptions are only examples. The reality is much more complex.

Coaches should constantly try to improve their own performance and bear in mind that their charges should enjoy their training sessions.

II. THE STARTING SITUATION: Where should the coach start?

A. Typical soccer aspects

Before he gives a training session the coach must think about what he wants to do, what he can expect to happen, and when and where the session is to take place. He must ask what he will need to take into consideration in actual practice.

He must keep the following aspects in mind:

1. The style of the club
- What is the style of the club?
- Has a policy, a work plan or a specific task been formulated by the club?
- How ambitious is the club?
- What is the club's selection policy?

2. The players
- How old are the players?
- Have they been selected?
- What level have they attained?
- How many players are involved?
- How many goalkeepers are there?
- How many players show up for practices/matches?
- What is the general mood?
- What sort of expectations are there?

3. Circumstances under which the coach must work
- How much time is available?
- What size and sort of field is available
- Are there enough good balls available?
- Are portable goals (full-size and small), posts, cones, etc. available?
- Are sufficient undamaged vests or shirts available?
- What are the weather prospects?
- Consult with other coaches who train teams, before, during, or after your training session.(shared facilities, equipment?)

4. Stage of the season or the learning process
- What stage of the soccer learning process has the group reached?
- How receptive to instruction and coaching is the group at this moment (vacation period, end of season, school activities, effects of weather, etc.)?
- What are the players facing in the near future?

If young players can't even tie their own laces, will they be able to understand the coach's technical and tactical tips, let alone apply them?

5. The coach himself
- Level of specialist knowledge.
- Experience as soccer player and coach.
- Interest in the group he is coaching.
- Style of instruction.
- Coaching skills and insight.
- Creativity.
- Attitude towards different players with different backgrounds.
- Attitude towards players with different levels of talent.
- Willingness to work with other coaches.
- Mood before the start of the session.
- Influence of events in previous session or match.

B. Example from daily coaching practice

Concerning 1. The style of the club
The players are selected from the club's whole 10-12 age group; the club has 4

teams in this age group.

The club's policy is that, when players reach this age, the best players should train with each other and try to finish as high as they can in their league competition. The club has a written policy documenting this, and there is an agreement that the coaches will apply this policy to the best of their ability. This policy is explained to new members so that they are aware of the views, objectives and style of the club. The coaches are engaged on a contract basis. The coaching coordinator is responsible for monitoring the proper functioning of the policy.

Concerning 2. The players

The squad consists of players in the 10-12 age group. 11 of them are second-year squad members and 5 are first-years. The first-years are selected on the basis of talent, their contribution to the team's overall performance, their ability to read the game and their motivation and keenness.

These are talented players who are very motivated and would rather train 3 or 4 times each week than on just the 2 occasions organized by the club. The team plays in the top division of the district, where it occupies second place and regularly wins by large scores. It therefore sometimes plays practice games or appears in tournaments against stronger competitive teams,so that the players can confront stronger resistance. One of the players is ill, so only 15 players will participate in the session. One of the two goalkeepers has hurt a finger, so although he can take part, he can't play in the goal. The first half of the season is almost over and the winter break is approaching. (During the break the squad trains once each week in the gym.) The squad has gone through a very good, instructive period and the general mood is excellent. The players are looking forward

to the 4 v 4 games in the hope of being selected for the district tournament. The squad expects that the training sessions will focus on improving positional play (a regular coaching theme at this age) and, in view of the forthcoming 4 v 4 club competition, games of 5 v 2, 3 v 2, 4 v 3 with goals, and 4 v 4.

The 4 v 4 competition takes place after the usual training session, and all the club's players in this age group participate.

Concerning 3. The coach

The coach is a former player who has acquired a certification as a youth soccer coach. He captained his college team and can talk long and lyrically about his soccer career. He repeatedly emphasizes the importance of positional play. This is his second year as coach of this age group.

He keeps a close eye on the 5 first-years. During the weekend he has prepared well for the training sessions and, especially, the 4 v 4 tournament.

A snapshot from the weekly 4 v 4 tournament.

Peter (11 years old): "One of the players in our team can do everything during the training session. But in real games he can't do anything right. The coach never says anything, and I don't think that's fair."

III. THE OBJECTIVE: What does the coach want to achieve?

A. Typical soccer aspects

The coach sets himself an objective for the training session. He lists what the players need to learn, what has to be improved, and what has to be reinforced. The comments under the heading "The Starting Situation" are of course useful here.

If a training session is to be effective, the coach must describe his objective as clearly as possible, so that he can then explain it to the players.

Important: A soccer problem must be clearly formulated before it can be dealt with effectively by a coach. The formulation must be very exact (see pages 41 - 43).

Sometimes objectives are pursued which are beyond the player's capacities - they are simply not old enough to achieve them. This results in an unenjoyable training session with a lot of frustration on the part of the players' and the coach. The

The coach sets objectives that are suitable for the players' level of development.

coach should always be aware of which objectives are suited to the different stages of the children's development.

To summarize, the coach should formulate his objectives for the training session on the basis of:

1. Insight into the starting situation
   • Age/talent/ambition of the players
   • What have we already learned?
   • What stage of the league competition are we in?

2. Knowledge of the typical characteristics of young players at certain ages.

3. Knowledge of soccer (analysis of the 3 main moments, and the associated objectives and starting points).

4. Knowledge, philosophy and attitude with respect to the process of teaching youngsters how to play soccer.

This age group must learn to play by taking part in basic games.

B. Example from daily training

The coach sets the following objectives:

Concerning 1. Starting situation
Improving positional play, and in particular improving the cooperation between the players. The players must have a joint idea of what everyone can contribute to the team effort from his own particular position, especially when the opposition has possession. The players know each other's strengths and weaknesses, but they must learn to communicate with each other.

Important:
> In the context of soccer, communication is always concerned with technical skills and the ability to read the game. It is more than just calling to each other and talking while on the pitch. It is also concerned with close observation, learning to recognize the pace of the ball, knowing when to sprint away suddenly from an opponent, when to stay at a distance from the ball, Learning the codes behind certain gestures (holding a hand up, pointing at the ground, nod of the head, etc.). Technique, Insight and Communication can be distinguished from each other but are always inseparable. They influence each other and are mutually interdependent (see Chapter 1)

Important:
> At this age the players, who previously thought that playing soccer was simply a matter of each individual trying to achieve something with a ball, can be taught the team aspects of the game. They must learn that they need each other in order to achieve a better soccer result.

Learning to master the ball... each player must have a ball!

Concerning 2.
Knowledge of young players

The objectives must be adapted to the typical characteristics of children at the various stages of their development. As has been mentioned before, at the age of 6-8 children must simply become familiar with the ball (how it feels, rolls, bounces) and the basic objectives of the game (scoring goals when you have the ball and preventing them when you don't).

Players in the 10-12 age group are ready to learn how to control the ball (technique) and how this is related to the objectives of the game (the 3 main moments). For example, many players have highly developed ball skills but need to learn to play more directly.

There are also some players who are not very good at controlling the ball in a tight situation. Or goalkeepers who are good at stopping shots but have a lot to learn about leaving their line and about recognizing situations when they must take charge and tell their defenders what to do.

Then there are players who are so hyper that they do everything too fast, and therefore make a lot of mistakes. They need to be taught to take the time to control the ball properly, take up a good position, and even hang back sometimes (patience is a virtue). The coach must formulate his objectives for the particular session, including individual objectives for specific players, within the context of the general objectives for this age group. The situation is therefore different for each situation and each group of players, so if a coach is to achieve anything, he must possess sufficient insight and knowledge.

Concerning 3. Knowledge of soccer
During this training session the coach wants to concentrate on defensive play, i.e. what to do when the opposition has the ball.

Richard (12 years old): "Our coach is very patient. He lets us find things out for ourselves. He often asks me what I did wrong, and what I should have done. During training sessions I work to eliminate the errors I made in the last match. The coach never scolds, so I always have the feeling that he wants to help. Our last coach was always scolding; nothing I did was right. I was always scared when a match was over, because I knew I would get the blame. I wasn't even then worst player. He just used to pick on me."

Players in the 10-12 age group often waste their energy by running futility after the ball.

The players don't recognize the right moment to go for the ball and they don't cooperate enough. Positional games and group games make considerable demands on the coach's knowledge and his ability to recognize specific situations.

Concerning 4. Knowledge, philosophy and attitude with respect to the process of teaching youngsters how to play soccer.

The above mentioned objectives were chosen on the basis of our knowledge of how children learn to play soccer. The essence of the matter is to confront children with typical soccer situations in which they repeat certain actions a large number of times and have a lot of fun while learning.

The coach has therefore geared himself to achieving the maximum return within the given time. His own attitude and approach is of considerable importance here. He must be patient, and he must be able to empathize with the players. He certainly should not regard his players simply as the passive clay from which he can mold his own success. He summarizes the objectives of the training session as follows: The players must learn to regain the ball when the opposition is in possession. Important aspects must be emphasized separately. There must be a joint concept of:

• The objective, i.e. to regain the ball (without giving away free-kicks).

• Where (in what part of the pitch) the various actions should take place.

• Who must play what role.

• What is required in terms of technical and physical ability.

A coach plays many roles.

IV. SOCCER TRAINING, IN PRACTICE: How should a coach do his job?

A. Typical soccer aspects

In training sessions a coach is confronted with a number of aspects which make demands on his knowledge, insight, attitude and skills.

The coach's knowledge, insight, attitude and skills:

1. Before:
- Be punctual, set the pitch up, get everything ready.
- Greet the players, record who is present, monitor the dressing room.
- Explain the objective, content, method and approach of the training session to the players.

2. During:
- Organization and sequence of events during the training session.

3. After:
- Supervise putting away the equipment used.
- Post-session discussion with the players, monitor the dressing room.
- Look forward to the next match or training session.

B. Example from daily training session

The coach has formed a picture of what he can expect from the training session, and what limiting conditions he will have to take into account, and he has a clear idea of the objectives of the session.

The important thing now is that the session proceeds as planned, and that the conditions are sufficient to achieve the set objectives. The best possible results must be achieved.

Concerning 1. Before

The coach arrives punctually and asks the equipment supervisor whether the new balls he requested last week have been bought yet. (There were too few size 4 balls to carry out certain drills.) It has also been agreed with the other coaches of the 10-12 age group that the hour after the training session will be devoted to the 4 v 4 tournament.

David (9 years old): "We have a new coach. I've learned a lot from him, probably because I enjoy his coaching. You can joke and laugh, but you always have to do your best. He always tells you that, but he never loses his temper. He is very demanding but you learn to play better. I have already scored three goals."

Equipment will be needed for this: posts to form goals, cones to mark out the playing areas, sufficient balls, and a blackboard on which to hang the match schedule and record the results.

The first players to arrive help to set up the equipment. The coach, as a former college player, is a sort of father figure, who gets the players to do what he wants without much fuss.

He starts by referring to an incident during the last match, then comments on the boots and laces of one of the players. He listens willingly as one of his players tells him about how he played for the school team, then raises his voice as the striker yet again takes his dirty, smelly boots out his bag with the excuse that he has not had time to clean them. He asks about the sick father of one of the boys, then uses the lemonade cups to illustrate how the third goal the team conceded during the last match arose. Finally he reminds the squad not to wear their shinguards too tightly, and that they are not allowed to play with long studs.

In short: the coach is there. He creates an atmosphere in which the squad wants to perform well. Today the training session will be followed by 4 v 4, with the other squads from this age group. The coach tells his players what he wants them to do and how. He uses an example from the previous match to illustrate how to improve.

"In this case you have to help each other better, especially when the opposition has the ball, and we have to make sure we win the ball back.

We'll play a positional game of 5 v 3, then 4 v 3, and finally 4 v 4."
The players listen closely and when the coach asks them a question they can answer it correctly in their own words.

This player is more than ready to improve his ability further to read the game.

Concerning 2. During the training session

The players warm up without supervision, as agreed at the start of the season. They do this in pairs, with one ball to each pair. 10 minutes are assigned to the warming up, which consists mainly of passing and receiving, alternately over short and long distances, moving towards the ball and away from it, and running into space and calling for the ball. A varied pattern of soccer skills.

The coach watches and occasionally makes a remark such as "You hit that too hard", "Play the ball when he asks for it", "Ask for the ball at the right moment, not when your partner hasn't got it under control", etc.

Positional game 5 v 3

The first practice game follows (a basic game). One player repeats what has to be improved, the coach helps him, and the first game is soon started.

A positional game of 5 v 3 has been chosen. The playing area is a fairly large rectangle, so the 3 defenders have to cooperate well and stay alert for the moment when they can win the ball back.

The methodology followed in this practice situation is:

- Firstly, start as quickly as possible within the confines of the described objectives.

- The three defenders don't win the ball often enough, they are brushed aside, so the coach stops the play and asks how often the defenders have managed to win the ball.

- He asks why they can't win the ball. The defenders answer that the pitch is too big. The coach responds "I think that you are not working together properly. Tom and Rob are running themselves into the ground but the three of you can't win the ball. The three of you must agree on the best moment to win the ball, and when to chase the ball and when not. You can force the attackers to one side in the corners and hem them in. You can make a feint towards the ball, like this. He then shows how to do it.

- The game is restarted. The coach intervenes a few times and stops the game, makes the players repeat their moves in slow motion, asks the players to demonstrate certain moves, and draws on an example from an important match that was recently on TV to illustrate his point more clearly.

- The coach makes the game more attractive for the 3 defenders (who swap roles with attackers) by giving them a concrete objective. For example, when they win the ball they can try to score immediately in a goal. The objective is to make it worthwhile to win the ball.

- The coach keeps emphasizing the proper execution of soccer skills, not only by the 5 attackers (passing, receiving, taking up position) but also the 3 defenders (feints, sliding tackles, tackles, staying on their feet, moving off the ball, mobility, alertness).

- If a free-kick is conceded the ball will certainly not be won back!

- The coach makes a special point of emphasizing the importance of watching the attackers closely; if they make a mistake this must be picked up immediately and the 3 defenders must go for the ball.

- When the coach stops the game he gives instructions with reference to what the players have shown him. He names names, gives examples, lets the players demonstrate or explain, and above all he shows that he is in charge and that he sees everything. No one can profit from an abstract theoretical dissertation.

- The coach can make the task of the 3 defenders easier or harder by manipulating the dimensions of the playing area, imposing restrictions on the attackers, or making the game competitive.

- The coach tries to realize his objectives by making the right remark at the right time and in the right tone of voice,

so that the players retain their enjoyment and motivation.

Positional game 4 v 3

The game of 5 v 3 is followed by 4 v 3 towards a full sized goal.

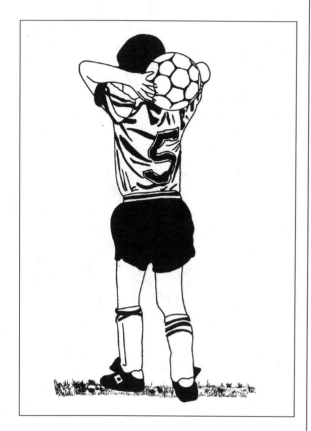

Robert (11 years old): "I played badly in my last game, because I could only think of my father. I couldn't do anything right. The coach took me out of the game, but didn't even ask why I was playing so poorly. In the dressing room I calculated that he has been in hospital two weeks now. I am going to visit him after this game."

Within the confines of the sa[m]e tives, the 3 defenders must now try to win the ball, but more imp also prevent the attackers from sc[o]

- The coach starts the game as qui[ck] possible. The attackers' positional too fast, allowing the defenders t[o] the ball too easily. The attackers therefore need to be coached in or[der] to make the game more interesting the defenders.

- The defenders are soon given a goal towards which they can direct the pl[ay] when they intercept the ball, for example by hitting a long ball to an (imaginary) advanced striker.

- The coach can make the defenders' task easier or harder in much the same way as before (changing the dimensions of the playing area, etc.), but can also use the offside rule.

- The coach ensures that the players swap roles regularly (defenders become attackers and vice versa), indicates the relevance to real matches, and tries to exploit the specific talents of a number of players.

4 v 4 game

A 4 v 4 game then follows, in which the aspects dealt with in the two preceding basic games (positional play, regaining possession) constantly recur.

The coach constantly points out the connections between the performance of the players in the previous positional games, and the last match, the remarks he has made and the situations in this 4 v 4 game.

mportant:

Didactic conditions

The coach constantly pays attention to a number of so-called 'didactic conditions'.

- He always relates his explanations to real situations, names names, and can call on a wealth of examples.
- He positions the group, or takes up position himself, in such a way that the players are not distracted by anything happening behind his back while he is talking (spectators, another training session, etc.)
- The group never stands facing the sun.
- The coach never talks into or across the wind, especially if his voice has to carry over a relatively large distance.
- The coach ensures that the problem he wants to solve becomes the players problem too. He may let the players reiterate it in their own words.
- He shows that nothing escapes his attention during the training session. He constantly 'reads' the play, if necessary out loud. He may also use a whistle.

Important: Presentation

The coach has a better chance of success in his role as instructor if he makes a good impression.

Obviously this also depends on how talented he is, but every coach can ensure that he has a neat track suit, good clean boots, and a smart appearance.

Good manners, patience, humor, enthusiasm and the ability to see things in perspective are all important in helping a coach to make a good impression. The coach must come over as being there for the players, not himself. Players must be able to look to the coach as a role model.

4 v 4 tournament

After the training session all the players in the 10-12 age group participate in a 4 v 4 tournament with an individual winner for the first time.

The players score individual points, and the player who scores the most is therefore the ultimate winner. The tournament will be repeated 3 times in the coming months.

The 4 players who score the most points in these tournaments will represent the club in the district tournament.

- The tournament is again explained briefly. All the pitches and equipment are ready.

- The players are assigned to their teams

for the first round and the start signal is given. Six players from the club's 16-18 age group act as field marshalls (one per pitch).

- The tournament proceeds, with each game lasting 10 minutes.

- The coaches run round and encourage the players, reminding them that the ball must be returned quickly into play, that they have to score, that the ball has to be won back quickly, etc.

- After completion each participant is given a memento.

Concerning 3. After the training session
Players and coach collect the equipment and put it away.

The coach makes sure that the players clean their boots before they go into the dressing rooms, that they use the dressing rooms and showers properly, that there is no petty quarreling about incidents during the training session, etc.

He then starts on the 'evaluation'.

V. EVALUATION: Was the training session useful?

A. Typical soccer aspects

In the soccer world, little attention has been paid to looking back on what has happened, how useful it was, and how the team performed. This is understandable, because all these matters are very subjective and depend on a number of factors.

However, it is a worthwhile exercise to analyze whether the players are on the right path and whether the training session proceeded as the coach wanted.

A number of recurring questions can serve as a guideline for the evaluation.

These are derived from the objectives of the learning process of youngsters.

1. Can the players be said to have played soccer?

2. Did the players learn enough (technical skills, insight and communication); was there a lot of repetition and did this have the desired effect?

3. Did the players enjoy themselves?

4. Did the coach take sufficient account of the characteristics of the group (age, ambition, talent)?

B. Example from daily training session

The coach discusses the training session with his players while they are clearing away the equipment and tries to discover whether they have learned what he wanted them to learn.

He stimulates them by recalling incidents from the session and making a few critical remarks about them. The players respond and give their views. One admits that a number of players sometimes gave up in certain situations.

In the dressing room the coach again asks what the objective of the training session was, and listens to the players' views. Naturally he does not act like a schoolteacher but tries to keep things more informal. The coach also singles out individual players for praise, a reprimand, a joke, etc. This too is part of creating a good atmosphere. Finally the coach looks forward to the next game, reminds the players when they have to meet, and then goes - tired but satisfied - for a refreshing shower.

The coach discusses the session and the 4 v 4 tournament briefly with the coaching coordinator, who is responsible for the team and runs through the selections for the Saturday games. The question of substitutions is also discussed: in the 10-12 age group it is important that everyone gets an equal chance.

The coach runs through the session again himself. He reviews his own role and makes notes on the progress of the individual players and the team as a whole.

Each minute of the training session is valuable

PICTURE	LECTURE	EXECUTION
Example, demonstrate, show	Explanation, information, clarification	Doing it yourself, practicing, trying, training, polishing the rough edges

Begin as quickly as possible!!!!

If the following steps are taken, the players can get started faster (no valuable time is taken up by long explanations)

1. Assign the players into groups (each with its own vests or shirts).

2. Assign the players' positions.

3. Explain the objective of the game.

4. Point out the boundaries of the field (cones, lines, boards, etc.; they should already be in place, or the players can be asked to put them in place).

5. Explain the rules of the game briefly, but clearly.

6. Ask for questions.

7. Answer the questions.

8. PLAY!

9. Interrupt the game or drill to adapt the obstacles:
   - larger/smaller playing area;
   - increase or reduce the number of players;
   - introduce new rules.

10. Finish off the practice game (just 1 minute to go/try to score the winning goal).

11. Short review/summary/conclusions about the drills carried out.

METHODOLOGY

Learning to play soccer: a question of progression, with lots of practice of course.

Learning to play soccer, like learning any other skill, is a step-by-step process. Each step is more difficult than the previous one, so that the players gradually acquire soccer maturity.

A coach must take account of not only a player's physical age, but also his "soccer age". An 8 year-old who has been playing soccer for 2 years will obviously be more advanced in his soccer development than a player of the same age who has just registered with the club, and the coach must adjust his objectives accordingly. After playing soccer for 2 years, a player is well on the way to understanding the basic games and therefore to being able to play properly. A player who has no experience

The objective has to be attainable.

of the game will have to start at the beginning (developing the basic technical skills).

The steps that a coach takes in order to teach youngsters to play soccer can be categorized under the heading of methodology, and are therefore a part of didactics.

Because the manipulation of obstacles to make drills harder or simpler is a science in itself, we treat this subject separately here.

1. What is methodology?

The following comments are intended to explain this more clearly:

* methodology is an element of didactics (= the science or art of teaching);

* fixed, considered manner of taking measures in order to achieve an objective;

* the path taken, and the steps along the path;

* manner of teaching/coaching;

* in accordance with a specific method, with the philosophy of the Dutch Soccer Association as the starting point;

* orderly, regulated;

* registration of step-by-step progress, the methodology of:
  * soccer games (from 1 v 1 to 11 v 11);
  * coaching:
  a. individual (from general technical remarks, through to the specific tasks associated with a specific position);
  b. team building (from general premises concerning the 3 main moments in a soccer game, through to team building).

2. The coach is an observer

As has already been mentioned, observation is the basis of coaching. What the coach sees and observes is the starting point of his coaching. He takes account of what the players do and what they are capable of doing (= teaching, improving, instructing, etc.).

The coach must possess knowledge, insight and skills in the following areas:
- playing soccer;
- child development;
- the learning process: how do youngsters learn to play soccer?
  - kinesiology;
  - didactics -> in which methodology (= theory of means) plays an important role;
- coaching.

3. Starting points and objectives of the various basic games

The basic games are intended to emphasize the objectives of a team when it has possession, when the opposition has possession, and when possession changes.

During these games the players are repeatedly confronted with a variety of soccer problems or situations which they have to solve. This is the great strength of basic games. By playing them, players learn to use their technique for the purpose of winning. Because no two soccer situations are exactly the same it is essential that players get lots of practice. Being able to hit an elegant pass with the side of the foot is well and good, but it is more important to be able to slot the ball accurately past the opposing players to the foot of a teammate. Young players must learn to apply their technique flexibly. In a given situation it may be necessary, for example, to place the non-kicking foot just behind the ball instead of alongside it in order to be able to pass to a teammate.

The methodology of the various game forms is important for teaching the players how to use all the necessary techniques flexibly. Making the obstacles faced by the players harder or easier is methodology.

Try to find a good balance between work and rest.

The following diagram illustrates this:

Goal Setting
Basic Form

Easy
More Difficult
Complex

Easy
Easier
Simpler

Resistance

- Number of teammates
- Number of opponents
- Size of the playing area
- Goal-orientedness
- Time
- Pressure
- Rules of the game

The above diagram relates to the basic game and the associated objectives. The game itself is not a "holy grail", but the objectives are. If players are unable to play the game properly, the coach must intervene to adjust the obstacles and change the game appropriately. The objectives must remain the same. The coach reads the game and decides whether measures need to be taken, and how to change the obstacles.

Methodology of the basic games

Basic games as derivatives of real matches

1 v 1

5 v 2

line soccer

4 v 4 (+ variations)

what is taught with regard to:

Technical skill

Insight and objectives

Communication

All coupled to the phase of development (age, experience, etc.).

The coach treats the basic games in accordance with a fixed procedure. The following elements recur frequently:

→ objective of the soccer element which is to be learned

→ suitable basic game:

- objective of the game
- organization of the game
- dimensions of the playing area
- number of attackers and defenders
- rules of the game
- competitive or practice game

→ the key learning rules

→ coach's observations (what the coach sees)

→ the coach analyzes the play, relates performance to objectives

→ the coach takes measures to improve the learning result in relation to the objective (methodical steps)

- see methodical list of questions

- a number of characteristic situations/pictures explained in terms of the problems faced

- the problem is formulated in such a way that the players (children) clearly grasp what is going wrong in relation to the objective (the players must look at it as their problem)

- besides giving general and/or specific instructions to the players during the game, the coach can modify the game and the obstacles. In short, he can take methodical steps, which may result in a different game but with the same objectives.

```
                    ┌─────────────────────────┐
                    │       Basic game         │
                    └─────────────────────────┘
                                 │
                                 ▼
            ┌───────────────────────────────────────────┐
            │                 Objective                  │
            │        "What has to be learned"            │
            └───────────────────────────────────────────┘
                                 │
                                 ▼
```

Coach's observations	Coach's knowledge, insight (+ problem)		Coach's measures (methodology)
Question: "Is the objective being achieved?"	Yes(1)	The game is flowing well, routine plays are good	→ Check technical execution. Incorporate competitive element.
	Yes(2)	This is too easy, the players are becoming careless	→ Make the obstacles more difficult or complex.
	No	There is no flow to the game. There are insufficient learning opportunities (repetitions). The players aren't motivated sufficiently.	→ Make obstacles easier, take measures to keep the game flowing.

Technique, insight and communication always belong together.

METHODOLOGY
from basic technique to real match

- **Basic skills = controlling the ball**

Dribbling	Passing	Receiving	Heading
Shooting	Kicking	Finishing	

- **Practice games with objectives -> learning to control the ball**

  - the ball: from objective to means

  objective: learning the feel of the ball, how it rolls, bounces, and how you can influence it

  means: using the ball to achieve an objective
  for example:
  - hitting a target by aiming well
  - keeping the ball at your feet in such a way that an opponent can't get it

- **Basic games with objective -> learning to control the ball in situations involving as many typical soccer obstacles as possible**

1 v 1	5 v 2	line soccer	4 v 4
	(see example)		

- **Scrimmages and competitive games**

- **Match**

Example:

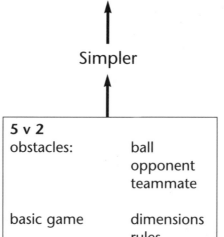

Basic skills
- passing and kicking
- controlling and dealing with the ball

↕

4 v 4

↕

3 v 1 → long, narrow playing area (rectangle)

↕

Simpler

↑

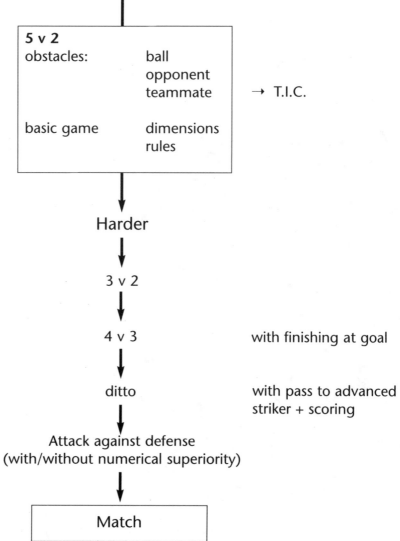

manipulating the
obstacles

5 v 2
obstacles: ball
                    opponent
                    teammate   → T.I.C.

basic game   dimensions
                        rules

↓

Harder

↓

3 v 2

↓

4 v 3   with finishing at goal

↓

ditto   with pass to advanced
                        striker + scoring

↓

Attack against defense
(with/without numerical superiority)

↓

Match

Besides the methodical steps in the basic games, a coach must also take a methodical approach to his coaching during matches and training sessions.

He must consider how to keep things clear and understandable for the players and himself. The list of questions below can help here. In principle it is a checklist for his work. It ranges from the basic precondition for learning (concentration), to the details of which players should take charge on and off the field in the oldest youth category.

With the youngest players, the emphasis of coaching will be on point 7, the use of technique. Points 4, 5 and 6 will be less prominent because the children are not yet ready for them. For more advanced players, these points are important in their training sessions and matches. The importance of each point depends on the level and experience of the players.

This player already knows that he has to look further than the ball at his feet.

Methodical list of questions

How does a coach give structure to his training sessions?

1 Concentration
- Are the children ambitious?
- Are the children interested in their tasks?

2 Making use of the objective
- Can the players understand it?
- Do they recognize the situation?

3 Organization, formation, positions
- Is the space used efficiently?
- Are the players positioned properly with respect to each other?

4 Players in their correct position
- Suitability for certain positions or functions.

5 Observation
- Are the players alert?
- Do the players see everything?

6 Communication
- Do the players communicate with each other? Are they geared to each other?
- Do the players "understand" each other?

7 Execution of specific tasks
- Does the action achieve anything? Is the objective achieved?
- Technical-motor skill execution -> quality/appearance.

8 Specific skills, talents, shortcomings
- Are these optimally exploited?
- Is everyone aware of them?

9 Distribution of tasks
- Who takes charge/accepts responsibility/takes a subordinate role?

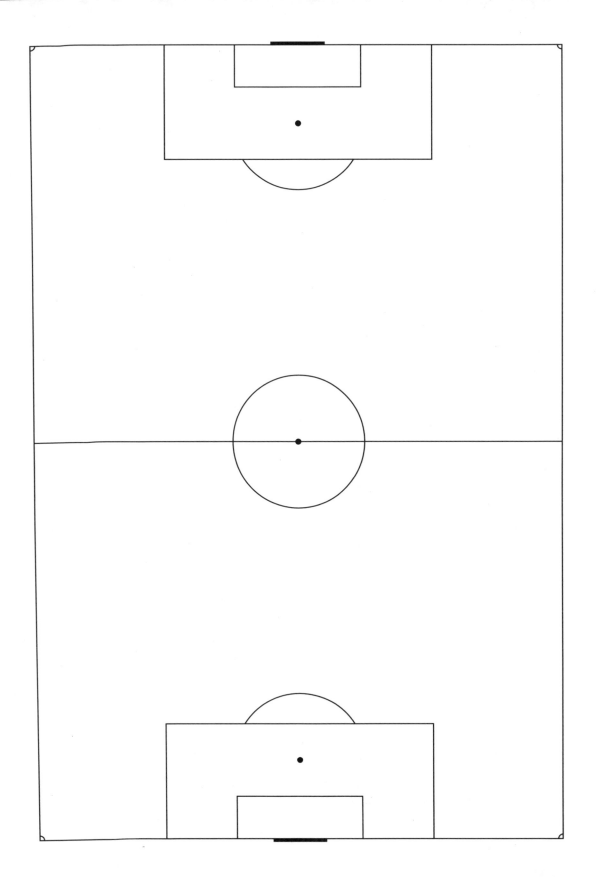

Match:_____

Date:_____

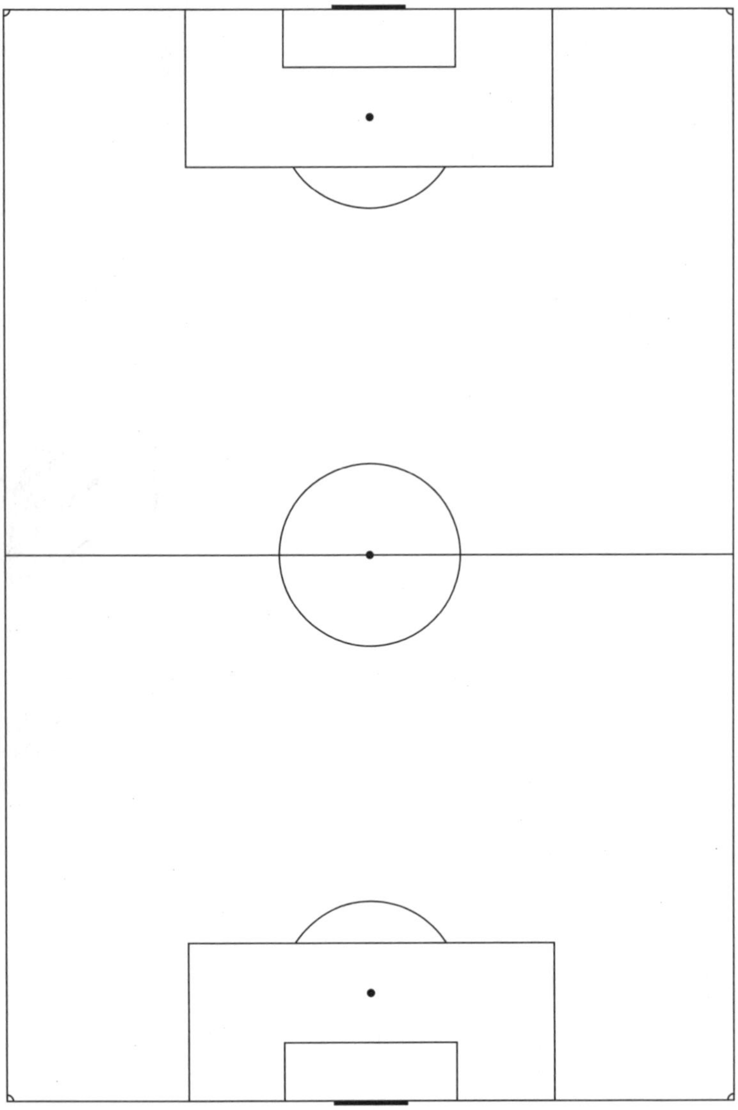

Line up:

1._____

2._____

3._____

4._____

5._____

6._____

7._____

8._____

9._____

10._____

11._____

Substitutes:

12._____

13._____

14._____

15._____

16._____

Focal points when in possession

Focal points when opponents are in possession